Chinese Cookery

Chinese Cookery

Deh-Ta Hsiung

WHSMITH
EXCLUSIVE
·BOOKS·

This edition produced exclusively for
W.H. Smith & Son Limited
Greenbridge Industrial Estate
Greenbridge Road
Swindon
Wiltshire SN3 3LD

Produced by
Bison Books Ltd
176 Old Brompton Road
London SW5 0BA

ISBN 0 86124 381 1

Printed in Hong Kong

The publishers would like to thank the
following for providing some of the props
used in the photographs

David Mellor
4 Sloane Square
London SW1 8EE

David Mellor
26 James Street
Covent Garden
London WC2E 8PA

David Mellor
66 King Street
Manchester M2 4NP

The London Architectural
Salvage & Supply Co Ltd
Mark St
London EC2A 4ER

McQueen's Florists and
Interior Landscaping
13 Pennybank Chambers
Great Eastern Street
London EC2A 3ET

Adams Antiques
Houghton Road
St Ives
Huntingdon
Cambridge PE17 4RG

Designer: David Copsey
Photographer: Clint Brown
Editor: Jane Laslett
Stylist: Andrea Brown
Home Economist: Hilary Newstead

Contents

Introduction

Travelling around the world today, I cannot help being impressed by the extent to which Chinese food and cooking has become established in almost every corner of the earth. This popularization of Chinese cuisine seems to have gathered a sudden and overwhelming momentum only during the last couple of decades. What has caused this sudden success of Chinese cuisine? The answer lies in the unique tradition and techniques of Chinese cooking, and in the inherent appeal of Chinese food and flavours to the palate. Also, Chinese food can be extremely economical as well as being highly nutritious, because most ingredients are cut into small pieces, then quickly cooked to retain all their natural goodness.

Trade and cultural exchanges between China and the outside world took place as early as the time of the Roman Empire, and over the centuries foreign influences and modern technology have affected nearly all walks of everyday life in China,

Cantonese Lobster in Black Bean Sauce (page 46).

except one – culinary art. In fact, foreign foodstuffs have been introduced into China since the dawn of history, but they all became integral ingredients of Chinese food.

Obviously, Chinese culinary art has gone through thousands of years of refinement and development, but the unique Chinese way of preparing and cooking food remains basically unchanged. Archaeological finds from the Bronze Age (beginning around 1850 BC) indicate the Chinese had utensils such as a bronze 'cleaver' for cutting food into small pieces, and a bronze pot, not dissimilar to the modern *wok*, for cooking in animal fat. We have written data to prove that as long ago as the Zhou Dynasty (12th century BC) the Chinese used soy sauce, vinegar, rice wine, fruit jam and spices as seasoning in their cooking, and that elaborate and complicated cooking methods were already being employed.

By the time of China's greatest sage Confucius (551-479 BC), an acknowledged gourmet as well, the importance of heat application and the blending of different flavours were emphasized in

Chinese cooking; the use of high, moderate or low heat, the blending of piquant, sour, salty, bitter or sweet flavours were all given their correct applications in order to achieve a harmonious whole. This theory of harmony is one of the main characteristics of Chinese cuisine to this day.

The main characteristics of Chinese cuisine

Chinese cooking has unique features. First, there is the Chinese division, when preparing and serving food, between *fan*, grains and other starch foods, and *cai*, meat and vegetable dishes. Grains in the form of rice or wheatflour (bread, pancakes, noodles or dumplings, etc), make up the *fan* half of the meal. Vegetables and meats (including poultry and fish, etc), cut up and mixed in various combinations into individual dishes constitute the *cai* half. A balanced meal must have an appropriate amount of both *fan* and *cai*. The fine art and skill of Chinese cuisine lies in combining various ingredients and the blending of different flavours for the preparation of *cai*.

The other distinctive feature is the harmonious blending of colours, aromas, flavours, shapes and textures in one single *cai* dish. The principle of blending complementary or contrasting colours and flavours is a fundamental one – the different ingredients must be mixed in a set pattern,

not indiscriminately, and is controlled, not casual. The cutting of ingredients is another important element. In order to achieve the proper effect, slices are matched with slices, shreds with shreds, cubes with cubes, chunks with chunks and so on. This is not only for the sake of appearance, but also because ingredients of the same size and shape require about the same amount of cooking time.

This complexity of inter-related elements of colours, flavours and shapes in Chinese cuisine is re-inforced by yet another feature – texture. A dish may have just one, or several contrasting textures, such as tenderness, crispiness, crunchiness, smoothness and softness. The textures to be avoided are sogginess, stringiness and hardness. The selection of different textures in a dish is an integral part of the blending of flavours and colours.

The desired texture or textures in any dish can only be achieved by the right cooking methods. In all the different methods, the correct degree of heat and cooking time are of vital importance.

Initial preparation and cooking techniques

A Chinese dish is usually made up of more than one ingredient; when a single item is served on its own it lacks contrast, therefore, there is no harmony. Some cooks like to mix contrasting flavours and unrelated textures, others prefer the matching of similar tastes and colours. Some wish the flavour of each ingredient to be preserved, others believe in the infusion of flavours.

To start with, you first choose the 'main' ingredient, then decide which type or types of 'supplementary' ingredients will go best with it, bearing in mind the colour, flavour and texture differences. For instance, if the main ingredient is chicken breast, which is white in colour and tender in texture, then a Chinese cook would choose something crisp like celery, which is also pale in colour, as the supplementary ingredient. Or, perhaps the cook would choose something more colourful like green or red peppers, both crisp, or something soft like mushrooms.

By combining different supplementary ingredients with the main one, and by the addition of various seasonings, it is possible to produce an almost endless variety of dishes without having to resort to unusual and exotic items. That is why a Chinese cook abroad can always produce a Chinese meal, even using only local ingredients. For the 'Chineseness' of the food depends entirely on *how* it is prepared and cooked, not *what* ingredient is used.

As mentioned, the cutting of various ingredients is an important element in Chinese cuisine. The Chinese cut their food into small, neat pieces before cooking, partly to conserve fuel and partly because small pieces of food are easier to serve and eat with chopsticks, as knives and carvers have not been used on Chinese tables since ancient times. Small pieces of food require only a short cooking time, thus retaining much of the natural flavours and nutritious value.

The size and shape of the cut ingredient must, first of all, be suitable for the particular method of cooking. For instance, ingredients for quick stir-frying should be cut into small, thin slices or shreds, never large, thick chunks.

Learn and understand the character of the ingredients, their textures and their colour changes. This is an important factor that helps you choose the appropriate cutting and cooking method.

Tender ingredients can be cut thicker than tough ones requiring longer cooking, and most meats change colour when cooked; chicken and pork become paler, while beef and lamb tend to go darker after being cooked.

After cutting, the next step in food preparation before cooking is marinating (this usually only applies to ingredients such as meats, poultry and fish, not to vegetables). The method is to marinate the white meats and fish in salt, egg white and cornflour, to preserve the natural delicate texture of the food when cooked in hot oil.

For red meats the basic marinade usually consists of salt, sugar, soy sauce, rice wine and cornflour. The purpose of this marinating is to enhance the flavour.

The two most important factors in cooking are degree of heat and cooking time. These two factors are so closely related to each other that it is impossible to separate them. This is why it is very difficult to give a precise cooking time in most recipes, because so much depends on the size and condition of the ingredients, and above all, on the type of the stove and cooking utensils being used.

All in all, there are well over 40 different distinct methods of cooking in Chinese cuisine. They fall roughly into the following categories:

Water cooking – Boiling, poaching and simmering

Oil cooking – Deep-frying, shallow-frying, stir-frying and braising

Fire cooking – Roasting, baking and barbecuing

Steam cooking – Steaming

Chopping up a whole chicken or duck for serving

1. Detach the two wings at the joints, then cut each wing into two pieces at the joint; discard the wing tips.
2. Detach the two thighs by cutting through the skin around the joints with a sharp knife or the tip of a cleaver. One at a time, separate the legs (drumsticks) from the thighs through the joints.
3. Lay the limbless bird on its side and separate the breasts from the backbone section by cutting down through the soft bone from the tail to the neck.
4. Carve away the skin and meat from the backbone section, cut into small bite-size pieces and arrange in a straight row along the centre of a serving platter (preferably oval).
5. Lay the bird breasts on the skin and remove the wishbone as well as the main breastbone by hand. Turn the meat over so the skin side is now facing upwards, and cut the two breasts in half lengthways, then chop each breast crossways into small, neat pieces. Transfer one half at a time, with the blade of a cleaver, to the serving platter and arrange on top of the backbone meat.
6. Chop the legs and thighs crossways into small bite-size pieces and arrange on each side of the breast halves. Arrange the two wings, one on either side, near the upper part of the breast meat, so that the original shape of the chicken or duck is now approximated.

Chinese regional cooking styles

The Chinese food tradition has changed very little during its several thousand year history, but what about the various styles of regional cooking? China is a vast country, with different climates and natural products varying from region to region and the cooking style reflects these divisions. Yet the fundamental character of Chinese cooking remains the same throughout the country: the Peking cooks in the north and the Cantonese cooks in the south all prepare, cook and serve their food in accordance with the *fan-cai* principle. What distinguishes one from the other is that in the north, the *fan* half is more likely to be wheat-flour food, while it is almost always rice in the south. Some of the cooking methods may vary a little from one region to another, and the emphasis on seasonings may differ. Sichuan in the west, for example, is renowned for its hot and spicy food, but basically food from all the regions is unmistakably 'Chinese'.

Obviously there are regional specialities, but with modern transportation, they are no longer confined to their place of origin. For example, the famous Peking Duck is just as popular as in Shanghai or Canton, or in London or New York!

Menu planning

As I mentioned, the main distinctive feature in Chinese cuisine is the harmonious balance of colours, aromas, flavours and textures, as well as shapes and forms, not only in a single dish but also in a course of different dishes. This aspect of serving Chinese food puzzles most Westerners, because the order of different courses served at a Chinese meal has no resemblance to the western convention of soup-fish-poultry-meat-cheese-dessert sequence.

The Chinese cooking tradition makes for a greater harmony of living, an aspect of Chinese cuisine which has often been overlooked: there is a great feeling of togetherness in the way the Chinese eat. We gather together round a table and partake of all the dishes which are placed on the table in communal style. Nobody is served just an individual portion in the western way, and chopsticks are used not only as eating implements, but also to help others to a choice piece – especially from a particularly tasty or special dish.

Due to the multi-course nature of a Chinese meal, eating and dining have always been very much a family or communal event; Chinese food is best eaten in this way, for only then can you enjoy a variety of dishes. An informal Chinese dinner served at home is essentially a buffet-style affair, with more hot dishes than cold served on the table at the same time, to be shared by everyone. Only at formal dinner parties or banquets are dishes served singly, or in groups, course by course. The order in which different courses or dishes are served depends more on the method of cooking and the way the ingredients are prepared before cooking, than on the actual food itself. That is why I have grouped the recipes under the general heading of cooking methods, which more or less determine the serving order, so as to simplify menu planning.

A typical dinner menu for 10-12 people would consist of 8-10 dishes served in the following order:

First course: 3-4 cold starters or an assorted *hors d'oeuvre* dish

Second course: 2-4 quick stir-fried, deep-fried or quick-braised dishes, always 'dry' rather than full of gravy. The exact number and variety of dishes are flexible, depending on the scale of the occasion, what was served before or what is to follow.

Main course: 1, 2, or 3 (or even 4!) 'big' dishes. These can be steamed, long-braised (red-cooked) or roasted, but usually consist of a whole chicken, duck, fish, and joint of meat. Again, the number and variety of dishes are flexible.

Rice course: noodles and dumplings are often served instead of, or as well as, rice at the end of a big meal.

Dessert: only served at formal banquets. Soup is often served for less grand occasions. Fresh fruit and China tea can be served at the end of a meal.

When it comes to planning the menu, just remember, as a rule, to allow one dish for one person, but two dishes should be enough for three to four people, three dishes for four to six people, four dishes for six to eight, and so on. Also remember the Chinese never serve an individual dish to each person; you all share the same dishes on the table. The only exception is when a light snack, such as a dish of *chow mein* or noodles in soup is served; each person is given his or her own portion.

What to drink with a Chinese meal

Do not serve tea or water with Chinese food. In China, soup is usually served throughout an everyday meal to help wash down the bulky and savoury food. When it comes to formal dinners or when entertaining, however, wine and spirits are an essential part of the fare. But the Chinese, in contrast to their sophisticated approach to food, are remarkably unfussy about alcoholic drinks. With the exception of true connoisseurs, the Chinese on the whole do not distinguish between wine, in which the alcoholic content is low, and a spirit, in which it is high. In the Chinese language, the word *jiu* or *chiew* means any fermented or distilled alcoholic beverage, beer included!

There are westerners who, although they would happily drink wine with highly spiced food from Italy, Spain or southern France, regard Chinese food and wine as incompatible. Personally, I always drink wine with my meals whenever possible.

Some people think only white wine goes well with Chinese food. Obviously a white is a perfect partner for cold starters and some lightly seasoned fried dishes, but for the more strongly flavoured dishes, you really need a wine that has plenty of body as well as bite. A good white wine of this calibre will cost you a small fortune, but there is a wide choice of smooth and fruity reds that are good value for money. By all means start your meal with a white, then go on to red if there are enough people eating to warrant opening more than one bottle. But if there are only two or three of you drinking, I recommend a light, fruity red such as a good beaujolais, Mâcon, Côtes-du-Rhône, a red from the Loire (Chinon, Bourgueil), California (cabernet sauvignon, pinot noir), Italy (Valpolicella, Bardolino) or Spain (Rioja). As for good quality whites, the best bet is to stick to the grape variety, such as riesling, sauvignon and chardonnay, be it from France, Germany, Italy, California or Australia!

A Chinese meal is served ready to eat – there is no last-minute carving on the table, or dishing out separate items such as meat, vegetables, gravy or sauce with all the attendant condiments; there is no long prelude when you all wait for everybody to be served before you start. At a Chinese table, when everyone is seated, the host will raise his glass and say *'gan-bei!'* (cheers!), or Bon appètit!

Clockwise from left: Fish with Black Bean Sauce (page 44); Fish Slice and Watercress Soup (page 26); Twice-Cooked Pork (page 60); Stir-fried Chicken and Cucumber (page 51); Plain Rice (page 74); Lychees.

Glossary

Agar-agar Also known as **Isinglass** (*kanten* in Japanese), a product of seaweed, sold dried in paper-thin strands or powdered form. Gelatine may be substituted.

Bamboo shoots Available in cans only. Once opened, the contents may be kept in fresh water in a covered jar for up to one week in the refrigerator. Try to get *Winter bamboo shoots*, which have a firmer texture.

Bean curd (tofu) This custard-like preparation of puréed and pressed soya beans is exceptionally high in protein. It is usually sold in cakes about 7.5 cm (3 inches) square and 2.5 cm (1 inch) thick in Oriental and health food stores. Will keep for a few days if submerged in water in a container and placed in the refrigerator.

Bean sprouts Fresh bean sprouts, from mung or soya beans, are widely available from Oriental stores and most supermarkets. They can be kept in the refrigerator for up to three days. Never use canned bean sprouts: they just do not have the crisp texture, which, apart from their high vitamin C content, is the main characteristic of this very popular vegetable. Another point to remember is not to over-cook them.

Bean sauce See: **Black bean sauce, Chilli bean sauce, Hoi Sin sauce,** etc.

Black bean sauce Salted black beans are crushed, then mixed with flour and spices, such as ginger, garlic or chillies to make a thick paste. It is sold in jars or cans, and once opened, the container should be kept in the refrigerator. Provided no grease, water or other organic matter come into contact, the sauce should last almost indefinitely.

Boiling Cooking by water, of which there are several methods:

(a) Rapid boiling over high heat. Thinly sliced or shredded ingredients are dropped into boiling stock or water and cooked for a very short time, usually no longer than it takes the liquid to return to the boil. Most soups are cooked this way.

(b) Boiling over medium heat under cover. This method is used for food that requires longer cooking time.

(c) Simmering over a low heat under cover.

(d) Blanching in boiling water. The food is then served with a dressing or sauce.

Braising The ingredients are first stir- or deep-fried (sometimes parboiled or steamed), then braised with seasonings and stock either over high heat for a short time, or over low heat for a long time. The latter is also known as **soy-braising** or **red-cooking**.

Cellophane noodles Also known as **Transparent vermicelli** or **Bean thread,** these are fine noodles made from mung beans, and sold in dried bundles weighing from 50g (2oz) to 450g (1lb). Soak in warm water for 5-10 minutes, or until soft, before use.

Chilli bean sauce Fermented bean paste mixed with hot chillies and other seasonings. Sold in jars, some are quite mild but some are very hot. You will have to try the various brands to see which is to your taste.

Chilli sauce Very hot sauce made from chillies, vinegar, sugar and salt. Sold in bottles, it should be used sparingly in cooking or as a dip. Tabasco sauce can be a substitute.

Chinese cleaver An all-purpose cook's knife that is used for slicing, shredding, peeling, pounding, crushing, chopping and even for transporting cut food from the chopping board to a plate or directly into the wok or pot. Chinese cleavers are available in a variety of materials and weights; choose a medium-weight, dual purpose cleaver known as the Civil and Military (*wen-wu dao*). It has a blade about 20-23 cm (8-9 inches) long and 7.5-10 cm (3-4 inches) wide. You use the lighter front half of the blade for slicing, shredding and scoring, etc; the heavier rear half of the blade is for chopping.

Chinese leaves Also known as **Chinese cabbage**, there are two types widely available varieties in supermarkets and greengrocers. The most commonly seen one has a pale green colour and tightly wrapped elongated head; about two-thirds of the cabbage is stem which has a crunchy texture. The other variety has a shorter and fatter head with curlier, pale yellow or green leaves, also with white stems.

Cooking oil In China, the most commonly used cooking oil is made from soya beans, peanuts, rape seeds or sunflower and cotton seeds. Lard (pork fat) or chicken fat are sometimes used but never butter or drippings.

Coriander Fresh coriander leaves, also known as Chinese parsley or *cilantro*, are widely used in Chinese cooking as garnishes.

Deep-frying Food is fried in a large quantity of oil in a wok; there are different variations of deep-frying:

(a) Dry deep-frying in hot oil over high heat; ingredients are not coated with batter or seasonings first.

(b) Soft deep-frying in hot oil over medium heat; ingredients are usually first coated with batter.

(c) Crisp deep-frying in hot oil over high heat; cooked ingredients (boiled, steamed or soft deep-fried) are then deep-fried for a very short time for crispness.

Dried Chinese mushrooms (*Lentinus edodes*) Highly fragrant dried mushrooms are sold in plastic bags; they are not cheap, but a small amount will go a long way, and they will keep indefinitely in an air-tight jar. Soak them in warm water for 20-30 minutes or in cold water for several hours, then squeeze dry and discard the hard stalks before use. Fresh mushrooms are quite different in fragrance and texture and are *not* a good substitute.

Dried shrimps These come in different sizes and have been salted and dried in the sun. They should be soaked in warm water for at least 20 minutes, then drained and rinsed before use. They will keep in the dry state in an air-tight container almost indefinitely.

Five-spice powder A mixture of star anise, fennel seeds, cloves, cinnamon and Sichuan pepper. It is highly piquant, so should be used very sparingly. It will keep in an air-tight container indefinitely.

Ginger root Fresh root ginger, sold by weight, should be peeled and sliced, finely chopped or shredded before use. It will keep for weeks in a dry, cool place. Another way of keeping it fresh is to peel, then place in a jar, cover with pale dry sherry, seal and store in the refrigerator. Ground ginger powder is not a good substitute.

Hoi Sin sauce Also known as **Barbecue sauce**, made from soy beans, sugar, flour, vinegar, salt, garlic, chillies and sesame seed oil. Sold in cans or jars, it will keep in the refrigerator for several months.

Monosodium glutamate Also known as 'taste essence' *(Veh t'sin),* a chemical compound widely used in restaurants to enhance the natural flavours of ingredients that are past their prime. Obviously, there is no need for it when cooking fresh food.

Oyster sauce A soya-based thick sauce used as a flavouring in Cantonese cooking. Sold in bottles, it will keep in the refrigerator for months.

Prawns In Britain, small prawns are usually sold already cooked, either in their shells or peeled. These are not really ideal for Chinese cooking; try getting the larger, uncooked variety sometimes known as king prawns, frozen when fresh, in their shells and headless. They should always be thoroughly defrosted before use.

Red bean paste This reddish-brown paste is made from puréed red beans and crystallized sugar. Sold in cans, the leftover content should be transferred to a covered container and it will keep in the refrigerator for several months. Sweetened chestnut purée can be substituted.

Rice wine Chinese rice wine, made from glutinous rice, is also known as 'yellow wine' *(Huang jiu* or *chiew),* because of its golden amber colour. The best variety is called **Shao Hsing** or **Shaoxing** from south-eastern China. A good dry or medium sherry is an acceptable substitute.

Salted black beans Very salty and pungent! Sold in plastic bags, jars or cans, they should be crushed with water or wine before use. Will keep almost indefinitely in a covered jar.

Sesame paste Also known as **Sesame sauce**, this highly aromatic, rich and tasty sauce resembles clay in colour and consistency. Sold in jars, stir well to make it into a creamy paste before use. Peanut butter creamed with sesame seed oil is a possible substitute.

Sesame seed oil Sold in bottles and widely used in China as a garnish rather than for cooking. The refined yellow sesame oil sold in Middle Eastern stores is not so aromatic, has less flavour and therefore is not a very satisfactory substitute.

Soy sauce Sold in bottles or cans, this most popular Chinese sauce is used both for cooking and at the table. *Light soy sauce* has more flavour than the sweeter *dark soy sauce,* which gives the food a rich, reddish colour.

Steaming Traditionally, the Chinese use a steamer made of bamboo which is placed inside a wok over boiling water. Now steamers made of metal, such as aluminium, are widely available in Chinese stores. A wok can also be used as a steamer as well; you fill the wok about one-third full with water and bring to the boil, then place the food in a heatproof dish or bowl, which is then placed on a rack inside the wok and covered with a dome-shaped lid.

Stir-frying By far the most frequently used cooking method in China. To stir-fry, preheat a wok or frying pan over high heat, add a small amount of oil and wait for it to get hot, then add the ingredients. Stir constantly and toss very quickly with seasonings. Timing and the temperature of heat are of utmost importance; overcooking will turn the food into a soggy mess. When correctly done, the food should be crispy and wholesome.

Water chestnuts Strictly speaking, water chestnuts do not belong to the chestnut family, they are the roots of a plant *(Eleocharis tuberosa).* Also known as *horse's hooves* in China because of their appearance before the skin is peeled off. They are available fresh or in cans; canned water chestnuts retain only part of the texture, and even less flavour than fresh ones. Water chestnuts will keep for about a month in the refrigerator immersed in a covered jar if you change the water every two or three days.

Wok The Chinese iron wok with a rounded bottom conducts and retains heat evenly, and, because of its shape, the food always returns to the centre, where the heat is most intense, however vigorously you stir. The wok is also ideal for deep-frying; its conical shape requires far less oil than the flat-bottomed deep-fat fryer, and has more depth (which means more heat) and more frying surface (which means more food can be cooked more quickly at one go). Besides being a frying pan, a wok is also used for braising, steaming, boiling and even smoking – in other words, the whole spectrum of Chinese cooking methods can be executed in one single utensil.

A new wok is either coated with machine oil or a film of wax to keep it from rusting. This coating has to be removed and a new coat of seasoning must be applied to the surface after cleaning, and be maintained throughout its life in order to keep the wok from rusting, as well as preventing food sticking to the bottom. After each use, wash the wok under hot or cold water, and *never use any detergents* as that will remove the seasoning.

Wonton skins Made from wheat flour, egg and water, these wafer-thin *wonton wrappers* are sold in 7.5 cm (3 inch) squares at Oriental stores. Can be frozen for up to six months.

Wood ears Also known as *Cloud ears.* A dried black fungus *(Auricularia polytricha).* Sold in plastic bags in Oriental stores, they should be soaked in cold or warm water 20 minutes, then rinsed in fresh water before use. They have a crunchy texture and a mild, but subtle, flavour.

Yellow bean sauce A thick paste made from salted, fermented yellow soya beans, crushed with flour and sugar. The sauce is sold in cans or jars, and once the can is opened, the contents should be transferred to a screw-top jar. It will then keep in the refrigerator for months.

Starters

You may be surprised to learn that the Chinese have an immense variety of dishes that are served as starters. Like hors d'oeuvres or antipasti, these dishes are generally small and simple, but they can be quite elaborate and even spectacular for a special occasion or formal dinner.

One of the advantages of these dishes is that, since most are served cold, they can be prepared and cooked well in advance – hours or even days beforehand. Another advantage is that when some of these dishes are cooked in fairly large quantity, any leftovers can be served again on another occasion, either on its own or with other dishes. Of course, most of these dishes are ideal for buffet-style meals or party food. If you are having a large dinner party, serve three or four starters before the stir-fried dishes and main course meals. Some of the dishes will be old favourites, many will be new to you.

The Chinese seldom eat raw vegetables for hygienic reasons because manure is used extensively as fertilizer in vegetable gardening. Most Chinese 'salad' dishes are precooked (usually by blanching or parboiling), then served cold with dressing. Obviously, vegetables grown in the West by modern methods are quite safe to eat raw.

Prawns with Sweet and Sour Sauce

Use fresh prawns if possible, otherwise serve ready-cooked ones cold with this delicious sauce.

450 g (1 lb) king prawns, defrosted if frozen
about 600 ml (1 pint) oil for deep-frying
2 spring onions, finely chopped
2 slices fresh root ginger, peeled and finely chopped
2 tablespoons soy sauce
2 tablespoons Shao Hsing rice wine or dry sherry
2 tablespoons sugar
1 tablespoon vinegar
about 125 ml (4 fl oz) stock (page 24) or water
2 teaspoons cornflour mixed with 1 tablespoon cold water
lettuce leaves, to serve
fresh coriander or parsley, to garnish

Wash and trim the legs off the prawns, without peeling, and then dry on kitchen paper.

Deep-fry the prawns in a preheated wok or frying pan for 30 seconds only; as soon as they start to turn pink remove with a slotted spoon.

Pour off the excess oil, leaving about 1 tablespoon in the wok. Add the finely chopped spring onions and ginger to flavour the oil for 1-2 seconds, then add the soy sauce, wine, sugar, vinegar and stock or water and bring the sauce to the boil, stirring constantly. Return the prawns, and thicken the sauce with the cornflour and water mixture, stir vigorously for a few seconds; when each prawn is coated with the glittering sauce, it is done.

Arrange the prawns neatly on a bed of lettuce leaves and garnish

with fresh coriander or parsley.

When eating, do not peel before putting the prawn in your mouth, but instead suck the sauce and extract the flesh off the shell at the same time. This is easily done if using chopsticks or fingers instead of a spoon and fork.

'Butterfly' Prawns

'Butterfly' prawns are simple to prepare and always warmly appreciated.
For best results, try to obtain uncooked giant prawns in their shells, known as king prawns. They are usually sold headless and are grey – they turn bright pink after cooking. King prawns are about 8-10 cm (3-4 inches) long, and you should get 18-20 prawns per 500 g (1 lb).

500 g (1 lb) king prawns in their shells, defrosted if frozen
1 tablespoon light soy sauce
1 teaspoon Sichuan peppercorns, crushed
3 tablespoons Shao Hsing rice wine or dry sherry
2 teaspoons cornflour
2 eggs, lightly beaten
4 tablespoons breadcrumbs
600 ml (1 pint) oil for deep-frying
lettuce leaves or watercress, to garnish
2-3 spring onions, thinly shredded, to garnish

Wash the prawns thoroughly, then dry with kitchen paper.

Pull off the legs with your fingers but leave the body shells and tails on. Using a sharp knife, carefully slit along the underbelly – the inner curve where you have just removed the soft legs – cutting about three-quarters of the way through the flesh.

Remove the black, sandy vein without cutting through the back shell.

Spread each prawn out, flesh side down, then tap once or twice gently with the flat side of the cleaver or knife to flatten the back a little, so that the flesh comes off easily from the shell when eating.

When you have prepared all the prawns, marinate them in a glass bowl with soy sauce, peppercorns, wine and cornflour for about 15-20 minutes. Any additional seasonings, such as garlic salt, paprika, mild curry powder or barbecue seasoning will enhance the flavour.

Heat the oil until very hot, then turn the heat off to let the oil cool down a little.

Meanwhile, lightly beat the eggs in a bowl and spread the breadcrumbs out on a flat plate.

Pick up a prawn by the tail and dip it in the egg, then roll it in the breadcrumbs before lowering into the oil – you can in fact do two at a time if you use both hands.

After a while, turn the heat on to high again and cook the prawns in batches until golden brown, then remove with a slotted spoon and carefully drain on kitchen paper.

To serve, arrange the prawns attractively on a bed of lettuce leaves or watercress, and garnish with thinly shredded spring onions, either raw or soaked for about 30 seconds in the hot oil you have just cooked the prawns in.

Butterfly Prawns.

Shanghai 'Smoked' Fish

**The fish is not actually smoked in this recipe; it acquires a smoky flavour from first being marinated in soy sauce and wine, then being deep-fried, and finally marinated again in a spicy sauce.
Fish that has been frozen is not suitable for this recipe, chilled fish only should be used.**

*450 g (1 lb) firm white fish steaks or cutlets, such as cod, haddock or halibut
3 tablespoons soy sauce
3 tablespoons Shao Hsing rice wine or Madeira
2-3 spring onions, finely chopped
2-3 slices fresh root ginger, peeled and finely chopped
2-3 tablespoons sugar
2 teaspoons five-spice powder
1 teaspoon salt
275 ml (½ pint) stock (page 24) or water
oil for deep-frying*

Dry the fish thoroughly with kitchen paper and leave the skin attached. Marinate in a glass bowl with soy sauce and wine for 2-3 hours, turning several times.

Remove the fish from the marinade, and add the finely chopped spring onions, ginger, sugar, five-spice powder, salt and stock or water to the marinade. Bring to the boil in a small saucepan, then reduce heat and simmer gently for 10-15 minutes. Strain through a fine sieve and set aside to cool.

Heat the oil in a preheated wok or deep-fat fryer until smoking hot. Fry the fish for about 5 minutes or until crisp and golden brown, turning once or twice during cooking. Remove the fish pieces with a slotted spoon and immerse in the sauce to cool for at least 3-4 hours. Remove from the sauce and lay out side by side on a dish to dry. Serve cold.

Note: The sauce can be stored in the refrigerator for 4-5 days and be used again when replenished with more seasonings.

Celery and Prawn Salad

In China, the celery would be blanched or parboiled for reasons of hygiene before serving, but I do not think it is necessary to do this in the West.

*1 tablespoon dried shrimps
1 tablespoon Shao Hsing rice wine or dry sherry
1 small celery
1 teaspoon salt
2 slices fresh root ginger, peeled and thinly shredded
1 tablespoon light soy sauce
1 tablespoon vinegar
2 teaspoons sesame seed oil*

Soak the dried shrimps in cold water for several hours or in warm water for at least 1 hour. Rinse and marinate in wine for 20-30 minutes.

Meanwhile, remove the celery leaves and outer tough stalks, then diagonally cut it into thin slices. Mix with salt and leave to stand for 10 minutes or so.

To serve, place the shrimps and wine and ginger on top of the celery, add soy sauce, vinegar and sesame seed oil. Bring to the table and toss thoroughly, then serve.

Poached Prawns with Cantonese Dip Sauce (left); Deep-Fried Prawn Balls on a bed of Crispy Seaweed with Dried Scallop Dressing (right).

Deep-fried Prawn or Crab Meat Balls

This is an excellent dish for a starter or buffet-style party when served crispy and dry. Alternatively, serve wet as a main course by braising in a little stock with vegetables.

*450 g (1 lb) uncooked prawns or crab meat, defrosted if frozen, and drained if canned
50 g (2 oz) fresh pork fat
8-10 water chestnuts, peeled
1 egg white, lightly beaten
1 tablespoon Shao Hsing rice wine or dry sherry
1-2 spring onions, finely chopped
1-2 slices fresh root ginger, peeled and finely chopped
salt and pepper
2 tablespoons cornflour
oil for deep-frying
lettuce leaves or Crispy 'Seaweed' (page 15), to serve*

Shell and devein the prawns, or remove the soft bones from the crab meat, then finely chop with the pork fat and water chestnuts. Mix together with the egg white, wine, spring onions, ginger, salt and pepper and cornflour. Blend well by stirring in one direction for 15-20 minutes until stiff. Chill for about 30 minutes before making into approximately 24 balls the size of walnuts.

Heat the oil in a preheated wok or deep-fat fryer until hot, then reduce the heat to low and let the oil cool down a little. Gently lower the balls into the oil, one by one, and deep-fry until golden, turning up the heat to moderate after a while.

Remove the balls with a slotted spoon and set aside if not serving at once. Just before serving, increase the heat to high and heat the oil to hot again, then put the balls back in the hot oil for a few seconds to crisp them. Serve hot on a bed of lettuce leaves or Crispy 'Seaweed'.

Alternatively, gently braise the balls in about 120 ml (4 fl oz) stock in a wok or pan for 5 minutes, then thicken the gravy with a little cornflour and water mixture. Serve on a bed of stir-fried vegetable such as mange-tout or Chinese cabbage.

Crispy 'Seaweed' with Dried Scallop Dressing

Hands up those of you who knew that this very popular 'seaweed' served in Chinese restaurants is, in fact, deep-fried cabbage! Since dried scallops are extremely expensive, by all means use dried shrimps as a substitute.

1 tablespoon finely chopped dried scallop
1 kg (2 lb) spring greens
1 litre (2 pints) oil for deep-frying
1 teaspoon salt
1½ teaspoons caster sugar

Soak the dried scallop in warm water, covered, for at least 30 minutes. Remove the stalks from the spring greens and thinly shred the leaves. Spread them out on absorbent paper to dry thoroughly. Drain the scallop and finely chop.

Heat the oil in a preheated wok or deep-fat fryer. When it is hot, turn off the heat for about 30 seconds, then add the spring greens in batches and turn the heat up to high again. Stir with cooking chopsticks and when the shreds start to float to the surface, scoop them out quickly with a slotted spoon or small sieve and drain on absorbent paper. Sprinkle the salt and sugar evenly all over the 'seaweed', then gently mix and garnish with dried scallop.

Serve hot or cold; this will remain crispy up to about 1 hour after cooking. Surprisingly, this 'seaweed' tastes like the real thing, and it also makes an ideal garnish for a number of dishes, particularly cold starters and buffet dishes (in which case you do not need either dried scallop or shrimps).

Poached Prawns with Cantonese Dip Sauce

If fresh prawns are unavailable, use ready cooked ones and serve cold; in that case all you need to do is make the dipping sauce.

500 g (1 lb) fresh unshelled prawns
1 teaspoon salt
1 litre (2 pints) water
2 spring onions, thinly shredded
2-3 slices fresh root ginger, thinly shredded
1-2 green or red chillies, seeded and finely shredded
2 tablespoons vegetable oil
2 tablespoons light soy sauce
1 tablespoon vinegar
2 teaspoons sesame seed oil

Defrost and wash thoroughly the prawns under cold running water. Poach them in a pan of salted boiling water for 1 minute, then turn off the heat and leave them in the water for another minute before removing and draining.

Place the shredded spring onions, ginger and chillies in a small heatproof bowl. Heat the oil until smoking, then pour it over the spring onions and set aside for 30 seconds. Add the soy sauce, vinegar and sesame seed oil and stir well.

To serve, each person picks up a prawn, peels off the shell, leaving the tail piece on as a handle, and dips the prawn in the sauce before eating.

Braised Eggs

For best results use more than one of the sauces from Soy-Braised Chicken (page 22), Fragrant Pork (page 21) or Braised Tripe and Tongue (page 17).

6 eggs
at least 600 ml (1 pint) sauce (see above)
water
soy sauce

Hard boil the eggs for 10 minutes, then carefully peel off the shells. Simmer in the sauce over moderate heat for 25-30 minutes, then add enough water and a little soy sauce to cover the eggs completely, if necessary.

Turn off the heat and leave the eggs to cool in the sauce for approximately 2-3 hours.

To serve, remove the eggs and drain for about 30 minutes, then cut them into quarters or thin slices and arrange on a plate either with garnishes or as part of assorted hors d'oeuvres.

Note: To save time, simply add the peeled, hard-boiled eggs to either Fragrant Pork or Braised Tripe and Tongue during the last stage of cooking.

Assorted Hors d'Oeuvres

Instead of serving several different cold dishes individually for the hors d'oeuvre course, it is always very impressive to arrange the various ingredients either in neat rows or into a pattern on a large dish (in the style of crudités). Garnish with cucumber, tomatoes, radishes, lemons or fresh coriander, bearing in mind that the visual appeal is intended to stimulate the appetite.

The complexity of assorted hors d'oeuvres should reflect the splendour of what is to follow, but a minimum of four different items is usually served: it should consist of the three meat dishes (fish, chicken and meat) and a vegetable. The selections may include Soy-Braised Beef (page 23), Fragrant Pork (page 21), Shanghai Soya Duck (page 22), Braised Eggs (page 16), 'White-Cut' Chicken (page 22), 'Smoked' Fish (page 14), Prawn or Crab Meat Balls (page 14), Poached Prawns with Cantonese Dip Sauce (page 15), Braised Tripe and Tongue (page 17), Pickled Vegetables (page 17) or Sweet and Sour Cucumber (page 17) for example. Only remember not to have more than one of the same type of food; the ingredients should be chosen for their harmonious contrast and balance in colour, aroma, flavour and texture.

Pickled Vegetables

Two important points to remember when pickling: first, make sure the jar has an air-tight lid; second, do not allow any grease to enter the jar at any stage.

2.5 litres (5 pints) boiled water, cooled
100 g (4 oz) salt
50 g (2 oz) brown sugar
1 tablespoon Sichuan peppercorns
5-6 red chillies
3-4 cloves garlic
5 tablespoons Chinese distilled spirit, or rum, brandy or vodka
4-6, or more, of the following: cucumber, carrot, radish, turnip,
*   cauliflower, broccoli, cabbage, celery, leek, sweet peppers, beans,*
*   root ginger and spring onions*

Put the water into a large, clean earthenware or glass jar with the salt, sugar, peppercorns, chillies, garlic and spirit.

Wash and dry the vegetables, trim and peel if necessary. Add to the jar and seal with an air-tight lid.

Store in a cool place and leave the vegetables to pickle for at least 4-5 days in summer, or 6-8 days in winter.

You can replenish the vegetables, adding a little more salt each time. If any white scum appears on the surface of the brine, skim it off then add a little sugar and more spirit.

Always use a pair of clean chopsticks or tongs to pick the vegetables out of the jar.

Chinese Cabbage Salad with Spicy Dressing

Chinese cabbage *(bok choy)*, also known as Chinese leaves, has pale-green leaves and long white stems with a crunchy texture. When not in season, substitute it with celery, cabbage or Webb lettuce.

1 small Chinese cabbage
1 small green pepper, cored and seeded
1 small red pepper, cored and seeded
1 teaspoon salt
½ teaspoon Sichuan peppercorns, crushed
1 tablespoon light soy sauce
1 tablespoon sesame seed oil
1 teaspoon chilli oil (optional)

Separate the cabbage leaves, discarding the tough outer leaves. Wash and dry thoroughly, then cut each leaf into large slices and place in a large serving bowl. Thinly shred the green and red peppers and place on top of the cabbage.

Sprinkle the salt and crushed peppercorns evenly all over the salad, then add the soy sauce and sesame seed oil. Toss and mix well, then leave it to stand for 15-20 minutes before serving. If using chilli oil or chilli sauce as part of the dressing, remember to add it only to the salad just before serving.

Clockwise from centre, Sweet and Sour Cucumber; Celery and Prawns Salad (page 14); Pickled Vegetables; Braised Eggs.

Sweet and Sour Cucumber

Select a dark green and slender cucumber; the fat pale coloured ones contain too much water and lack flavour. This is a Sichuan recipe.

1 slender cucumber, about 30 cm (1 foot) long
1 teaspoon salt
1 tablespoon sugar
2 teaspoons vinegar
1-2 teaspoons sesame seed oil

Halve the cucumber lengthways, then cut across diagonally into thick chunks, without peeling. Marinate the cucumber with salt and sugar for 10-15 minutes, mixing well.

Add vinegar and sesame seed oil just before serving.

Note: This salad can be served on its own, or used as a decorative garnish for other dishes.

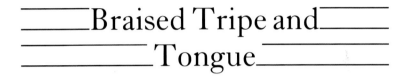

Braised Tripe and Tongue

This is a surprisingly delicious starter; try this recipe even if you do not usually enjoy tripe.
You can use the stomach of either ox, sheep or pigs, and the tongues of either lamb, pigs or ox for this recipe; you do not have to use *both* tripe and tongue at the same time, they can be cooked on separate occasions

1 kg (2¼ lb) tripe and/or tongue, defrosted if frozen
2 tablespoons vegetable oil
2 spring onions
2-3 small pieces fresh root ginger
4 star anise, or 1 teaspoon ground aniseed
3 cinnamon sticks
2 teaspoons Sichuan peppercorns
5-6 cloves
1 tablespoon sugar
125 ml (4 fl oz) Shao Hsing rice wine or sherry
2 teaspoons salt
5 tablespoons soy sauce
600 ml (1 pint) stock (page 24) or sauce from Soy-Braised Chicken
*   (page 22) or Fragrant Pork (page 21)*
sesame seed oil (optional) and finely chopped spring onions, to
*   garnish*

Pat the tripe dry with kitchen paper.

Heat the oil in a saucepan and lightly brown the tripe on both sides, then add the remaining ingredients and tongues, if using, and bring to the boil.

Reduce the heat and gently simmer, covered, for about 1 hour. Turn off the heat and leave the tripe and/or tongues to cool in the sauce for 3-4 hours before removing.

Cut the tripe and tongues into thin slices.

Garnish with sesame seed oil and finely chopped spring onions just before serving.

Note: Any leftovers can be tightly wrapped and stored in the refrigerator for up to 4-5 days. The sauce should be strained and can be reused; it will keep for many weeks if stored in the refrigerator in an air-tight container.

Peking Sesame Seed Prawn Toasts

You may be surprised to learn that this delicious dish, very popular with restaurants serving Peking-style food, originated in Hong Kong.

225 g (8 oz) uncooked prawns, defrosted if frozen
50 g (2 oz) fresh pork fat
salt and pepper, to taste
1 egg white, lightly beaten
1-2 spring onions, finely chopped
1 slice fresh root ginger, peeled and finely chopped
1 tablespoon Shao Hsing rice wine or dry sherry
2 teaspoons cornflour
6 large slices white bread, crusts trimmed
100 g (4 oz) white sesame seeds
1 litre (2 pints) oil for deep-frying
shredded lettuce or Crispy 'Seaweed' (page 15), to serve

Shell and devein the prawns and dry thoroughly, then chop with the pork fat until they form a smooth paste. Mix with the salt and pepper, egg white, spring onions, ginger, wine and cornflour.

Spread the sesame seeds evenly on a large plate or a baking tray. Spread the prawn mixture very thickly on the top of each slice of bread, then place, spread-side down, on the surface of the sesame seeds, pressing gently so each slice has a good coating of seeds.

Heat the oil in a preheated wok or deep-fat fryer until hot. Fry the bread slices, spread-side down, 2 or 3 slices at a time, for about 2 minutes or until they start to turn golden; turn over and fry for a further minute or so. Remove and drain on kitchen paper.

Cut each slice into 6 fingers or 4 triangles, and serve hot on a bed of lettuce leaves, or better still, on a bed of Crispy 'Seaweed'.

For a big party, you can make a large quantity of the mixture days ahead, then freeze until the day of the party. They can be cooked straight from the freezer.

Bean Sprout Salad

Use the freshest bean sprouts available – although they may be kept in the refrigerator for a day or two, they soon become discoloured and lose much of their crunchy texture.

450 g (1 lb) fresh bean sprouts
1 teaspoon salt
2 spring onions, thinly shredded
2 tablespoons light soy sauce
1 teaspoon sugar (optional)
1 tablespoon vinegar
1 tablespoon sesame seed oil

Wash and rinse the bean sprouts in a basin of cold water, discarding the husks and other bits and pieces that float to the surface. It is unnecessary to top and tail each sprout – that would be too time consuming!

Place the sprouts in a large bowl or a deep dish, add the salt, toss and let stand for 10-15 minutes.

Just before serving, place the spring onions on top of the sprouts, add sugar, if using, soy sauce, vinegar and sesame seed oil. Bring to the table and toss thoroughly, then serve.

Note: A little finely shredded fresh red chilli, carrot or cooked ham can be added as garnish to give this salad an extra colour as well as extra flavour.

18

Hot and Sour Cabbage

This is another Sichuan recipe, but is very popular throughout China. Choose a round, pale-green cabbage as fresh as possible with a firm heart; the white Dutch variety is a good substitute, but do not use loose-leafed dark-green cabbage.

1 pale-green or white cabbage, about 700g (1½ lb)
3-4 tablespoons vegetable oil
5-6 small dried red chillies, (more, if you like it hot!)
10-12 Sichuan peppercorns
1 teaspoon salt
2 tablespoons sugar
2 tablespoons vinegar
1 tablespoon soy sauce
1 teaspoon sesame seed oil, to garnish

Wash the cabbage in cold water, then tear the leaves by hand into small pieces, each about the size of a matchbox.

Heat the oil in a preheated wok or large pan until it starts to smoke. Swirl the wok around so that the oil covers about two-thirds of the surface, then add the chillies and peppercorns to flavour the oil. (Hold your breath for a few seconds, or you will need a gas mask!) Before they burn, quickly add the cabbage and stir until it starts to go limp – this will take about 1 minute.

Add the salt and continue stirring about 1 minute more, then add the sugar, vinegar and soy sauce. Stir for 20-30 seconds to allow the sauce to blend, then add the sesame seed oil.

Serve hot or cold.

Green Beans and Red Pepper Salad

Green beans, also known as French beans or dwarf beans, should not need stringing if they are young and fresh.

225 g (8 oz) green beans
1 teaspoon salt
1.1 litres (2 pints) water
1 medium, or 2 small, red peppers, cored and seeded
1 teaspoon finely chopped fresh root ginger
1 teaspoon sugar
1 tablespoon light soy sauce
2 teaspoons sesame seed oil

Wash the beans and top and tail, if required, then snap each bean in half; very fine dwarf beans can be left whole. Blanch in a pan of salted boiling water, then quickly pour into a colander and rinse under cold water until cool. Drain.

Place the beans in a serving dish. Thinly shred the red peppers and add them to the beans together with the ginger, sugar, soy sauce and sesame seed oil.

Mix and toss well just before serving.

Note: A fresh green or red chilli, thinly shredded or finely chopped, can be added to the dressing instead of, or as well as, the ginger, if desired.

Clockwise from left: Peking Sesame Seed Prawn Toasts; Hot and Sour Cabbage; Green Beans and Red Pepper Salad; Bean Sprout Salad.

Spicy Mutton

Lamb and beef can be substituted in this Mongolian recipe.

1 kg (2¼ lb) filleted leg of mutton or lamb
3-4 spring onions, each tied into a knot
4 slices fresh root ginger, peeled
1 tablespoon Sichuan peppercorns
5-6 star anise
1 tablespoon salt
4 tablespoons Shao Hsing rice wine or sherry
oil for deep-frying
lettuce, finely chopped spring onions and sesame seed oil, to garnish

Cut the meat along the grain into 4-5 long strips. Marinate in a glass bowl with the spring onions, ginger, Sichuan peppercorns, star anise, salt and wine for 1-2 hours (longer if possible).

Place the meat in a heatproof bowl and cover with foil. Place in a hot steamer and steam for about 2 hours. (Or, place the bowl over a pan of boiling water and simmer for 2 hours.) Remove the meat from the bowl and cool until required.

Heat the oil in a preheated wok or deep-fat fryer until smoking. Deep-fry the meat strips for 4-5 minutes, then remove and drain. Cut the meat into thin slices and neatly arrange on a bed of lettuce leaves with the garnishes.

Chicken and Ham Salad with Mustard Sauce (left); Crystal-Boiled Pork with Crushed Garlic and Sauce (right).

Chicken and Ham Salad with Mustard Sauce

This is a well-known starter from northern China. It is extremely simple to prepare, and most delicious to taste.

25 g (1 oz) agar-agar or isinglass
1 tablespoon mustard powder
175 g (6 oz) cooked boned chicken meat, skinned
100 g (4 oz) cooked ham
½ cucumber, about 15 cm (6 inches) long
1 tablespoon light soy sauce
1 tablespoon vinegar
1 tablespoon sesame seed oil

Soak the agar-agar in warm water until soft, which should take no more than ½ hour. Meanwhile, mix the mustard with a little cold water to form a thin paste and set aside for 30 minutes for the flavour to mellow.

Drain and dry the agar-agar, then cut the shreds into matchstick-sized lengths. Shred the chicken, ham and cucumber to the same size. Arrange all the ingredients neatly in separate layers on a serving dish: pile the cucumber shreds on a bed of agar-agar, then add the chicken and the ham on top like a pyramid.

Blend the mustard paste with the soy sauce, vinegar and sesame seed oil. Pour the sauce evenly over the salad. Mix the dressing and the salad together at the table just before serving so that you do not disturb the carefully arranged pattern.

Fragrant Pork

In China, belly pork is known as 'five-flower meat' because, when viewed in cross-section, the alternate layers of lean meat and fat form a pretty pink and white pattern.

1 kg (2¼ lb) belly of pork
2 spring onions
2-3 small pieces fresh root ginger, peeled
1 teaspoon salt
4 star anise, or 1 teaspoon ground aniseed
3 cinnamon sticks
1 dried tangerine peel
8 cloves
100 g (4 oz) rock candy or crystal sugar
175 ml (6 fl oz) Shao Hsing rice wine or dry sherry
125 ml (4 fl oz) soy sauce
lettuce leaves, to garnish

Cut the pork into 15×7.5×5 cm (6×3×2-inch) chunks. Place it in a large saucepan with all the remaining ingredients and enough cold water to cover the meat. Bring to a rolling boil and keep the heat fairly high for about 2 hours, adding a little water from time to time if necessary.

To serve, remove the meat from the sauce and cut it into thin slices like bacon rashers. Serve on a bed of lettuce leaves.

Note: The sauce can be stored for 4 or 5 days in the refrigerator and reused for cooking other meat, chicken or eggs. Leftover pork can be used in other dishes (page 72).

Crystal-Boiled Pork with Crushed Garlic Sauce

Another dish from Shanghai, and like the Cantonese 'White-Cut' Chicken (page 22), it is very simple and easy to make.

1 kg (2¼ lb) leg of pork, boned but not skinned

Sauce:
2 cloves garlic, crushed and finely chopped
2 spring onions, finely chopped
1 teaspoon finely chopped peeled fresh root ginger
1 teaspoon sugar
4 tablespoons soy sauce
2 teaspoons sesame seed oil, or 1 tablespoon chilli oil

Place the pork, in one piece, tied with string if necessary, in a pot of boiling water to cover. Return to a rolling boil and skim off the scum, then reduce heat and simmer gently, covered, for 1 hour. Turn off the heat and leave the pork in the water for at least 3-4 hours before removing to cool, skin side up, for 4-6 hours.

For the best flavour and to preserve the moist texture, do not cut the meat until just before serving.

To serve, cut off the skin and any excess fat, leaving only a thin layer of fat on top, like a ham joint, then cut across the grain, into small thin slices. Arrange neatly in rows on a plate.

Mix together all the sauce ingredients and pour over the pork, then serve.

Shanghai Soya Duck

This was one of my favourites as a cold starter in China, but, unfortunately, I have never seen it on any restaurant's menu in the West.

2 kg (4½ lb) duckling
2 teaspoons salt
2 tablespoons red rice flour
5-6 star anise, or 1 teaspoon ground aniseed
2-3 cinnamon sticks
2 litres (4½ pints) water
3-4 spring onions, each tied into a knot
3-4 pieces of fresh root ginger, peeled
100 g (4 oz) rock candy or crystal sugar
5 tablespoons Shao Hsing rice wine or brandy
2 tablespoons light soy sauce

Clean the duck well then blanch in boiling water. Remove and rinse under cold running water, then pat dry. Rub the cavity with the salt.

Wrap the red rice flour, star anise and cinnamon in a muslin bag and drop into a pot of fresh water; bring to the boil and boil the bag for 15-20 minutes, when the water should turn red. Remove the bag and put the duck in the water with the spring onions, ginger, sugar, wine and soy sauce. Reduce the heat and simmer for 1 hour until the sauce is reduced by half. Turn the heat up to high again and baste the duck constantly with the sauce. When the sauce is reduced by half again, remove the duck, drain well and set aside to cool.

To serve, chop the duck into small bite-size pieces (page 7), either on its own, or as part of an assortment of hors d'oeuvres.

Cantonese 'White-Cut' Chicken

There are a number of variations for this famous Cantonese dish. The most important point to remember is you should never use a frozen chicken or an old boiler.

1.5 kg (3½ lb) free-range chicken
2-3 slices fresh root ginger, peeled
2-3 spring onions
3 tablespoons Shao Hsing rice wine or dry sherry
1 tablespoon salt

Sauce
3 tablespoons light soy sauce
1 teaspoon sugar
1 tablespoon sesame seed oil
2 spring onions, finely chopped

Clean the chicken well and place in a large pot with enough water to cover. Add the ginger, spring onions and wine, then bring to the boil and skim off the scum. Cover with a tight-fitting lid and simmer over low heat for 10-15 minutes *only*. Add the salt, replace the lid, take the pot off the heat and let the chicken cook gently in the hot water for 4-6 hours or until the liquid is cool; *do not* lift the lid while you wait. In fact, you should put something heavy on top of the lid to make sure that no heat escapes.

To serve, remove the chicken and drain well. Chop into 20-24 bite-size pieces, then reassemble on a dish (page 7).

Mix together the sauce ingredients and evenly pour all over the chicken, then serve.

Soy-Braised Chicken

This is a Cantonese recipe that can be prepared and cooked well in advance and served cold. This dish is ideal for buffet-style parties.

1.5 kg (3½ lb) free-range chicken
1 tablespoon ground Sichuan peppercorns
1-2 tablespoons finely minced peeled fresh root ginger
3 tablespoons dark soy sauce
2 tablespoons light soy sauce
3 tablespoons Shao Hsing rice wine or dry sherry
2 tablespoons brown sugar
3-4 tablespoons oil
600 ml (1 pint) stock (page 24) or water
lettuce leaves, to garnish

Clean and dry the chicken, then rub inside and out with the ground Sichuan peppercorns and minced ginger (dried ginger powder should *not* be used). Marinate the chicken with soy sauce, wine and sugar in a deep glass bowl for at least 3-4 hours (longer if possible), turning it every 30 minutes.

Heat the oil in a preheated wok or large pot until smoking and brown the chicken all over. Add the marinade and stock or water, then bring it to the boil and reduce the heat and simmer gently for 40-45 minutes, covered, turning 3-4 times during cooking; be careful not to break the skin.

Remove from the heat but leave the chicken in the sauce for at least 1-2 hours before removing it to cool completely. Chop into bite-size pieces (page 7) and arrange neatly on a bed of lettuce leaves. Pour over it a little of the sauce and serve. To add more colour, decorate the edge of the plate with cucumber and tomato slices. The remaining sauce can be stored in the refrigerator for several months, and can be used to make Braised Eggs (page 16).

Shanghai Soy a Duck.

Sichuan Bon-Bon Chicken

This very popular dish from Sichuan is also known as Bang-Bang Chicken in some restaurants, so called because the chicken meat is tenderised by being banged with a stick *(bon)*.

1 kg (2¼ lb) young chicken
1 litre (2 pints) water
1 tablespoon sesame seed oil
lettuce leaves, to garnish

Sauce
2 spring onions, finely chopped
1 teaspoon sugar
2 tablespoons soy sauce
1 teaspoon chilli oil
1 teaspoon ground Sichuan peppercorns
1 teaspoon sesame seeds
1 tablespoon sesame paste or peanut butter creamed with a little
  sesame seed oil

Clean the chicken well and dry thoroughly. Bring the water to the boil, add the chicken and cook, covered, for 40-45 minutes, turning over once or twice. Remove the chicken and put it in a pan of cold water for 1-2 hours to cool, then remove, drain and pat dry. Brush on a coating of sesame seed oil and leave to dry for another 10-15 minutes.

Shred the lettuce leaves and place on a serving dish. Carve off the chicken legs, wings and breasts and pull the meat off the bones. Pound the chicken with a rolling pin to loosen the meat from the carcass, then tear the meat into shreds with your fingers. Place on top of the lettuce leaves.

Mix together all the sauce ingredients and pour over the chicken. Mix and toss at the table just before serving.

Shanghai Soy a Duck.

Soy-Braised Beef

This is a Muslim dish from north China; mutton can be cooked by the same method.

750 g (1½ lb) shin of beef
2-3 spring onions
3-4 slices fresh root ginger, peeled
3-4 tablespoons brandy
water
2-3 tablespoons oil
1 teaspoon salt
1 tablespoon sugar
1 teaspoon five-spice powder
4-5 tablespoons soy sauce
1 teaspoon sesame seed oil, to garnish (optional)

Place the beef, spring onions and ginger in a saucepan with the brandy and just enough water to cover the meat. Bring to the boil, skim off the scum and gently simmer, covered, for 45 minutes.

Remove the beef and set aside to cool. Meanwhile, heat the oil in a wok or pan and brown the beef all over. Add the salt, sugar, five-spice powder, soy sauce and a little of the cooking liquid. Stir and cook for about 5 minutes before returning the meat and sauce to the saucepan. Return to the boil, then reduce the heat and simmer, covered, for 30-40 minutes.

Remove the beef to cool. Just before serving, slice it thinly and garnish with a little sesame seed oil, if liked.

Soups

Soup is not regarded as a separate course in China, except at formal occasions and banquets. At an everyday meal in Chinese homes a simply made soup, usually a clear broth with a small amount of thinly sliced or shredded vegetables and/or meat, is served with all the other dishes throughout the meal. This provides the liquid for washing down bulky and savoury foods. At more formal banquets or dinners soup is sometimes served as a separate course at the end of the meal.

If you wish, you may of course serve any of the following soups as a separate course. Noodles in soup is often served as a snack, but this is included in the final chapter.

If stock is unavailable, a Chinese cook will stir-fry the ingredients first, then add them to boiling water with seasonings.

If you decide to use a chicken or beef stock cube as a substitute, remember to reduce the amount of seasonings in the recipes as bouillon cubes are always extremely salty. However, home-made stock is far superior in flavour, and is worth making if you have the time.

Clear Soup (Basic Stock)

This is the first item a Chinese cook prepares in the kitchen each morning. Besides being the basis for soup making, a good stock is also used instead of water for general cooking whenever liquid is required.
Any stock left over at the end of the day should be refrigerated; it will keep for up to 5 days. Alternatively, freeze the stock in small containers (ice-cube trays are ideal for this), then defrost whatever amount is needed.

1 kg (2¼ lb) chicken pieces, excluding breast meat
1 kg (2¼ lb) pork spare-ribs or bones
1 large piece fresh root ginger
3-4 spring onions
5 litres (10 pints) water
4-5 tablespoons Shao Hsing rice wine or dry sherry (optional)

Trim excess fat from the chicken and pork, then place in a large saucepan. Add the unpeeled and chopped ginger, onions and water. Bring to the boil and skim off any scum. Simmer, uncovered, for at least 2 hours; by then the liquid should be reduced by about one-third.

Strain the stock, discarding the chicken and pork, then add the wine and return to the boil.

Simmer for 5 minutes, then it is ready to be used as stock or, with the addition of seasonings, such as salt and pepper, to be served as a clear soup, like a consommé.

Allow about 180 ml (6 fl oz) per person.

Sliced Lamb and Cucumber Soup

A delicious soup which originated in Peking. This is a variation of the Hot and Sour Soup but it is much simpler to prepare.

225 g (8 oz) boned leg of lamb
1 tablespoon Shao Hsing rice wine or dry sherry
1 tablespoon light soy sauce
1 teaspoon sesame seed oil (optional)
½ cucumber, about 15 cm (6 inches) long
600 ml (1 pint) stock (page 24)
1 tablespoon vinegar
salt and pepper

Trim off any excess fat from the lamb and thinly slice. Cut into pieces about the size of a large postage stamp. Place in a glass bowl and marinate with the wine, soy sauce and sesame seed oil, if using, for 20-25 minutes, turning occasionally.

Halve the cucumber lengthways, then cut into thin slices, without peeling.

Bring the stock to a rolling boil, add the lamb and stir to separate, then return to the boil. As soon as the soup starts to boil again, add the vinegar, cucumber and seasonings, then pour the soup into a heated tureen and stir well. Serve hot.

Spinach and Bean Curd (*Tofu*) Soup

This is a nutritious and extremely popular soup in China, where it is given the rather poetic name of 'Emerald and White Jade Soup'. When spinach is not in season, simply substitute another tender green vegetable, such as cabbage, lettuce or watercress.

1 square cake bean curd (tofu)
100 g (4 oz) spinach leaves, excluding stems
600 g (1 pint) stock (page 24)
1 tablespoon light soy sauce
salt

Cut the bean curd into 12 small slices about 0.5 cm (¼ inch) thick. Wash the spinach thoroughly, separating the leaves.

Bring the stock to a rolling boil, then add the bean curd and spinach and simmer for about 2 minutes. (Lettuce or watercress requires less than 1 minute cooking.) Skim the surface to make it clear, add the soy sauce and salt and stir well. Serve hot.

Sliced Lamb and Cucumber Soup.

百怒定天下
千秋爭是非
無德遠

Fish Slices and Watercress Soup

This is a delicious soup from northern China. Plenty of white pepper makes this an ideal dish for cold winter nights. The watercress can be replaced with cabbage, lettuce or spinach.

225 g (8 oz) white fish fillet, such as plaice or lemon sole
1 tablespoon cornflour
1 egg white, lightly beaten
1 bunch watercress
about 600 ml (1 pint) oil for deep-frying
600 ml (1 pint) good stock (page 24) or water
1 teaspoon finely chopped fresh root ginger (optional)
1 tablespoon vinegar
salt
white pepper
finely chopped spring onions, to garnish

Cut the fish into slices about the size of a matchbox. Dust with cornflour, then coat with egg white. Wash the watercress thoroughly. (If using cabbage, lettuce or spinach, thinly shred the leaves.)

Heat the oil in a preheated wok or deep-fat fryer. Fry the fish slices for about 1 minute or until lightly golden, then remove with a slotted spoon and drain well on kitchen paper. Pour off the oil, add the stock or water to the wok or a saucepan and bring to the boil. Add the ginger, vinegar and fish and return to the boil, then add the watercress, salt and pepper. Simmer for about 1 minute, pour into a warm tureen, garnish with spring onions and serve hot.

Chinese Cabbage and Mushroom Soup

Traditionally, after the meat and skin have been taken from the Peking Duck (page 42), its carcass is made into a soup with cabbage and mushrooms to be served at the end of the meal. This is really only practical for the restaurants, since there will always be a spare duck carcass to make the soup with, long before you have finished eating; at home you will have to wait for a good hour or two before the soup is ready for serving. Therefore, I suggest that you keep the carcass for another day, and make the soup with ready-made stock.

1 duck carcass, plus giblets, if available
2 small pieces fresh root ginger
4-6 dried Chinese mushrooms, soaked in warm water for 30-45 minutes
500 g (1 lb) Chinese cabbage
salt and pepper
fresh coriander sprigs, to garnish

Break up the carcass, place it with the giblets and any other bits and pieces in a large pot. Cover with water, add the ginger and bring to the boil, skimming the surface. Cover and simmer for 45-60 minutes.

Squeeze the mushrooms dry, discard the stalks and cut into thin slices.

Wash the cabbage and cut into 2.5 cm (1 inch) slices. Add the cabbage and mushrooms to the soup about 10-15 minutes before serving. Adjust seasonings and garnish with fresh coriander.

Seafood and Asparagus Soup

Chinese Cabbage and Mushroom Soup (left); Seafood and Asparagus Soup (right).

The original recipe from southern China calls for abalone. I think you will agree that abalone is an acquired taste besides being extremely expensive, so I have substituted scallops.

100 g (4 oz) peeled prawns
100 g (4 oz) shelled scallops
50 g (2 oz) honey roasted ham
100 g (4 oz) asparagus
900 ml (1½ pints) stock (page 24)
salt
finely chopped spring onions, to garnish

Ideally, use uncooked prawns if you can get them; otherwise add the ready cooked prawns to the soup at the very last moment. If the prawns are large, then cut each into 2 or 3 pieces. Cut each scallop into quarters and finely dice the ham.

Discard the tough asparagus stems, and diagonally cut the tender spears into short lengths.

Bring the stock to the boil, add the asparagus and parboil for 2-3 minutes. Add the ham, prawns and scallops with the salt. Return to the boil and simmer for 1 minute at the most. Serve hot, garnished with spring onions.

Note: When asparagus is not in season, use any other tender greens such as mange-tout, lettuce heart or watercress. Mange-tout will only need to be boiled for 1-2 minutes; lettuce heart and watercress less than 1 minute.

West Lake Beef Soup

This is a Cantonese soup named after a famous beauty spot outside Canton.

100 g (4 oz) beef steak, such as rump
2 teaspoons soy sauce
1 tablespoon Shao Hsing rice wine or dry sherry
1 teaspoon sugar
1½ tablespoons cornflour mixed with 2 tablespoons cold water
600 ml (1 pint) stock (page 24) or water
1 egg, lightly beaten
100 g (4 oz) shelled peas
a few drops of sesame seed oil
salt and pepper
finely chopped spring onion, to garnish

Coarsely chop the beef not quite as small as mince. Place in a glass bowl and marinate with the soy sauce, wine, sugar and about 1 tablespoon of the cornflour and water solution.

Bring the stock or water to the boil, very slowly pour in the beaten egg, stirring constantly. Add the peas and return to the boil, then add the beef and stir to separate the pieces.

Thicken the soup with the remaining cornflour and water mixture, and add the sesame seed oil and salt and pepper. Pour the soup into a tureen and garnish. Serve hot.

Chicken and Mushroom Soup

There are two different versions for this soup – either clear or thick. The clear version is more authentic, but you must use a good stock as the basis; the thick soup is more of a Westernized version, in which it is not necessary to use stock at all; just add plenty of egg whites and cornflour to plain water.

100-150 g (4-5 oz) chicken breast meat, skinned and boned
3-4 dried Chinese mushrooms, soaked, or 100 g (4 oz) fresh mushrooms
600 ml (1 pint) stock or water
2-3 egg whites (optional)
1 tablespoon cornflour
1 tablespoon cold water (optional)
salt
a few drops sesame seed oil
finely chopped spring onions, to garnish

Thinly shred the chicken meat. Squeeze dry the mushrooms, discard the hard stalks and cut into thin shreds; if using fresh mushrooms, wash but do not peel, and thinly slice.

Bring the stock or water to the boil. Meanwhile, stir the egg whites with your fingers or chopsticks until slightly runny and blend to a smooth paste with the cornflour and water mixture. Add the chicken and mushrooms to the stock or water, stir and return to the boil, then very slowly pour in the egg whites if using, stirring constantly. Now add salt to taste and thicken the soup with the cornflour and water mixture if using, stirring. Sprinkle over sesame seed oil and garnish with spring onions. Serve hot.

Hot and Sour Soup

This surely must be the second most popular soup after Sweetcorn and Crab Meat Soup served in Chinese restaurants. Most people associate it with Sichuan or Peking cooking, but like so many other famous dishes, it is more or less a national favourite in China. There are a number of regional variations, but the ingredient you need in order to produce the traditional version is bean curd (tofu).

3-4 dried Chinese mushrooms, soaked
100 g (4 oz) pork fillet or chicken breast meat, skinned and boned
1 cake bean curd (tofu)
50 g (2 oz) bamboo shoots
900 ml (1½ pints) stock (page 24) or water
1 tablespoon Shao Hsing rice wine or dry sherry
1 tablespoon soy sauce
1 tablespoon vinegar
1 tablespoon cornflour mixed with 2 tablespoons cold water
salt
white pepper

Squeeze dry the mushrooms and discard the stalk. Thinly shred the meat, mushrooms, bean curd and bamboo shoots. Bring the stock or water to the boil, add the meat and mushrooms, stir and return to the boil, then add bean curd and bamboo shoots and simmer for 2-3 minutes. Add the wine, soy sauce and vinegar. Stir gently while adding the cornflour and water mixture to thicken the soup. Add salt and plenty of white pepper, stir well and serve hot!

Sweetcorn and Crab Meat Soup

This very popular Cantonese soup originated in Chinese restaurants abroad, but it has recently been introduced into China and is well received there.

100 g (4 oz) crab meat, thawed if frozen and drained if canned
1 teaspoon finely chopped fresh root ginger
2 egg whites
2-3 tablespoons milk
1 tablespoon cornflour
900 ml (1½ pints) stock (page 24)
225 g (8 oz) can creamed sweetcorn
salt and pepper
finely chopped spring onions, to garnish

Flake the crab meat, then mix with the ginger. Beat the egg whites until frothy, then add the milk and cornflour and beat again until smooth. Blend in the crab meat.

Bring the stock to the boil, add the sweetcorn and return to the boil. Stir in the crab meat and egg white mixture, adjust seasonings and stir gently until well blended. As soon as the soup thickens, sprinkle with the spring onions, then serve at once.

Note: Coarsely minced chicken breast meat can be used instead of crab meat for this soup; the method is the same.

Sliced Pork and Vegetable Soup

This is a basic recipe for 'meat and vegetable' soup – beef, chicken, liver or kidney can be substituted for the pork. You can also use any green vegetables, such as spinach, Chinese leaves, green cabbage, mange-tout, lettuce or watercress.

100 g (4 oz) lean pork fillet
100 g (4 oz) green vegetable
600 ml (1 pint) stock (page 24) or water
1 tablespoon Shao Hsing rice wine or dry sherry
1 tablespoon soy sauce
salt and pepper

Thinly slice the cut pork into postage-stamp sized pieces. Trim and wash the vegetable, then cut into 2.5cm (1 inch) pieces.

Bring the stock or water to a rolling boil, add the meat and stir to separate, then boil for only 30 seconds. Remove the meat with a strainer or sieve. Holding the strainer over the boiling soup, slowly pour the wine and soy sauce over meat and into the soup. Skim the soup, and add the vegetable and return to boil. Simmer for 1-1½ minutes depending on the type of greens used; cabbages take about 2 minutes, while lettuce and watercress will require 30 seconds at the very most. Place the meat and seasonings in a tureen, pour the broth and vegetables over and stir well. Serve hot.

Left to right, Hot and Sour Soup; Sweetcorn and Crabmeat Soup; Sliced Pork and Vegetable Soup.

Egg Drop Soup

The Chinese name translates as 'Egg-Flower' Soup. This must be about the simplest method of making a soup – and most economical as well, since a single egg can serve up to six people! However, do not be so frugal just this once. Be a devil and use TWO eggs to serve four people!

600 ml (1 pint) stock (page 24)
2 eggs
salt
1 tablespoon finely chopped spring onions, to garnish

Bring the stock to a rolling boil.

Meanwhile, lightly beat the eggs with chopsticks or a fork, and add a pinch of salt.

Pour the eggs very, very slowly into the boiling stock, stirring constantly.

Add salt to taste, and garnish with the chopped spring onions. Serve immediately.

Main Course Dishes

The dishes that constitute the main courses in the serving sequence of a conventional Chinese dinner require a longer cooking time than stir-fried dishes; they usually consist of large joints or, in the case of fish and poultry, are often cooked whole. Most of these dishes can be prepared and cooked well in advance, avoiding any last minute rush if you are planning a big dinner party.

Some of these dishes are even interchangeable with the hors-d'oeuvres and buffet dishes. The distinctions are often difficult to define: the general rule is that certain dishes are best served cold, therefore they are grouped together in the first chapter while a number of long-braised, roasted and steamed dishes are best served hot, therefore they are placed in the main course section.

Obviously, there is no need for you to do a full scale Chinese meal, with all the trimmings, to serve these 'big' dishes, as we call them in China. Almost all the dishes in this chapter can be served independently, and, furthermore, most of them blend extremely well with Western food.

The widely used method for long-cooking is soya-braising or 'red-cooking'. There are a number of variations to this technique, the most common one being just like stewing: the ingredient is first half cooked by frying, deep-frying, steaming or boiling, then slowly cooked with soy sauce, sugar, wine and spice or spices as the primary seasonings.

Most Chinese home kitchens are equipped with simple stoves but no ovens; a Chinese family only expects to eat roasted food in restaurants. Since very few kitchens in the West are without an oven, there is no reason why you should not cook your own Peking Duck (page 42) or Cha Shao Roast Pork (page 33), for example, at home. The method is really quite simple as you will see by following the recipes in this book.

After quick stir-frying, the Chinese method of steaming must appear simple and easy, as it requires minimum preparation and hardly any cooking skills. Yet, to achieve the perfect result, it is important that you are acquainted with a few inter-related basic and essential points.

(1) The quality and texture of the food is vital. It must be fresh and tender.

(2) The ingredients should not be too large or bulky.

(3) The water must be kept on a rolling boil all the time.

(4) Never place the food into a cold steamer.

Traditionally, the Chinese used a bamboo steamer, which is placed *inside* a wok over boiling water but today, steamers made of aluminium are widely available.

A wok can be used as a steamer as well – you place the food in a heatproof bowl or dish, which is then placed on a rack inside the wok, one-third filled with boiling water, and covered with a dome shaped lid. The main drawback of the conventional Western steamers is their size. They seldom exceed 20 cm (8 inches) in diameter for home kitchens, which is not wide enough to accommodate even a small fish 30-55 cm (12-14 inches) long, for example.

Sichuan Steamed Beef.

Sichuan Steamed Beef

In China, we often use bicarbonate of soda to tenderize the beef; this is unnecessary in the West since beef is better.

700 g (1½ lb) beef steak, such as rump, topside or silverside
1 teaspoon sugar
2-3 tablespoons Shao Hsing rice wine or dry sherry
1 tablespoon light soy sauce
2 tablespoons chilli bean paste
1 teaspoon finely chopped peeled fresh root ginger
2-3 spring onions, finely chopped
1 teaspoon freshly ground Sichuan pepper
1 tablespoon oil
75 g (3 oz) ground rice
225 g (8 oz) cabbage leaves or green beans
sesame seed oil and finely chopped spring onions, to garnish

Thinly slice the beef into pieces not much bigger than a matchbox. Marinate with the sugar, wine, soy sauce, chilli bean paste, ginger, spring onions, pepper and oil, for at least 45 minutes.

Roast the ground rice in a dry frying pan over moderate heat, stirring, until golden brown and aromatic. Line the rack of a bamboo steamer with cabbage leaves or green beans. Coat each slice of beef with the ground rice, then arrange in neat rows, slightly overlapping, on top of the vegetables.

Steam vigorously in a wok of boiling water for about 15 minutes, depending on how tender the beef is; the more tender, the less steaming time. Garnish with sesame seed oil and finely chopped spring onions. Serve hot directly from the steamer.

Crispy Roast Pork

Ideally, the 'five-flower meat', which is the Chinese name for belly of pork, should be in one piece; if that is not possible, then at least keep the meat in large chunks.

1 kg (2¼ lb) belly pork in one or two large pieces
2 teaspoons salt
1 tablespoon five-spice powder
lettuce leaves, soy sauce and chilli sauce, to serve

Dry the skin well and make sure that it is free from any hairs and score with several deep-cuts. Rub the salt, then the five-spice powder all over the pork, and set aside to stand, covered with skin-side up, for at least 3 hours – the longer the better, say 6-8 hours, if possible.

Preheat the oven to 240C/475F/Gas 9. Place the pork, skin-side up, on a rack in a roasting pan on the middle shelf of the oven and roast for 15-20 minutes. Reduce the oven temperature to 200C/400F/Gas 6 and cook for a further 20-25 minutes or until the skin has become crackling. Remove from oven to cool a little before cutting it into small, bite-size pieces. Serve on a bed of lettuce, and have a range of different dipping sauces on the table for people to choose.

Note: Leftover pork can be used for a number of other dishes.

Braised Spare-Ribs in Brown Sauce

This is one of my family's favourites – and I must modestly admit I invented this recipe myself.

700 g (1½ lb) pork spare-ribs
½ teaspoon salt
½ teaspoon ground Sichuan pepper
1 tablespoon sugar
1 tablespoon light soy sauce
2 tablespoons Shao Hsing rice wine or brandy
2 teaspoons cornflour
2-3 tablespoons oil
2 cloves garlic, crushed
2-3 spring onions, cut into short lengths
2 tablespoons crushed yellow bean paste or Hoi Sin sauce
225 ml (8 fl oz) stock (page 24) or water
1 large or two small green peppers, seeded and cored and cut into small pieces

Trim the excess fat from the spare-ribs, then chop each rib into small bite-size pieces. Marinate with the salt, pepper, sugar, soy sauce, wine and cornflour for 30-45 minutes, stirring once or twice.

Heat the oil in a preheated wok or large frying pan until smoking. Flavour the oil with the garlic and spring onions, then add the spare-ribs and bean paste, stirring constantly until the ribs are light brown. Add the stock or water, bring to the boil and continue stirring for 5-10 minutes until the sauce is reduced to almost nothing. Add the green peppers and blend well. Serve hot.

Red-Cooked Pork with Bamboo Shoots

Traditionally, the Chinese use the cheap cuts of pork such as belly or hand with rind for this dish. If you are too calorie-conscious, by all means use a less fatty cut of meat, but remember the rind enriches the sauce, and the bamboo shoots will absorb most of the excess fat.

700 g (1½ lb) pork with rind
2 spring onions, cut into short lengths
2 slices peeled fresh root ginger, cut into small pieces
2-3 tablespoons oil
1 tablespoon sugar
1 teaspoon five-spice powder
2-3 tablespoons Shao Hsing rice wine or dry sherry
1 tablespoon light soy sauce
3 tablespoons dark soy sauce
about 450 g (1 lb) bamboo shoots

Cut the pork into 2.5 cm (1 inch) cubes.

Heat a saucepan or pot and pour in the oil. When hot, add the sugar and stir until lightly brown. Add the pork, spring onions and ginger, stirring until well blended, then add five-spice powder, wine, and soy sauce. Continue stirring, then add enough water to cover the meat and bring to the boil. Reduce the heat and gently simmer, covered, for 1 hour.

Cut the bamboo shoots to cubes about the same size as the pork, and add to the pan, stirring gently to mix and blend. Cook for a further 20-25 minutes. Serve hot.

Cha Shao Roast Pork

***Cha Shao (Char Siu* in Cantonese) is a specialized Cantonese method of roasting meat. Although often called Barbecued Pork in some restaurants, it is in fact strips of pork roasted quickly in the oven after a long period of marinating. When cooked, a coat of maltose syrup (or honey) is applied to the meat, then it is returned to the oven for a few more minutes so that the finished product looks reddish brown and slightly charred, particularly around the edges.**

1 kg (2¼ lb) fillet of pork

Marinade:
½ teaspoon salt
1 tablespoon sugar
1 tablespoon yellow bean paste
2 tablespoons Chinese spirit, brandy, whisky or rum
1 tablespoon light soy sauce
2 tablespoons dark soy sauce or Hoi Sin sauce
1 teaspoon sesame seed oil
lettuce or Chinese cabbage, to serve
2 tablespoons honey dissolved with a little water, to garnish

Cut the pork into strips about 18-20×4×2.5 cm (7-8×1½×1 inch).

Mix together the marinade ingredients in a shallow earthenware dish and marinate the pork, covered, for at least 12 hours at room temperature, or 24 hours in the refrigerator, turning occasionally.

Preheat the oven to 220C/425F/Gas 7, and place a baking pan filled with about 600 ml (1 pint) boiling water at the bottom to create hot steam so that the meat remains moist when cooked. This will also catch any drips during cooking.

Take the pork strips out of the marinade, reserving the marinade, and drain well. Put the tip of an S-shaped hook through one end of each strip, then hang the strips on the top rack, making sure they dangle freely, not touching each other, and that they are not too near the water.

Alternatively, the pork strips can be placed flat on a wire rack. Still use the pan of boiling water.

Roast for 15-20 minutes, then baste with the marinade and reduce the oven temperature to 180C/350F/Gas 4. Cook for a further 20-25 minutes.

Remove the meat from the oven (but do not turn the heat off yet) and let it cool down for 2-3 minutes, then brush the strips with the honey and return them to the oven and cook for 4-5 minutes more to crisp the outside a little and turn it into a rich golden colour with slightly charred edges.

To serve, remove the meat from the hooks and cut the strips across the grain into slices, then arrange them neatly on a bed of lettuce or Chinese cabbage leaves.

Bring the remaining marinade to the boil with the drippings and the pan of water and gently simmer for a few minutes, then strain into a jug to be used as a sauce or gravy.

Any leftover Cha Shao will keep in the refrigerator for 4-5 days if wrapped tightly in clingfilm. For best flavour and to preserve the moist texture, try to keep the strip whole – slice just before serving. It can be used as a part of an Assorted Hors d'Oeuvres (page 16), or as one of the ingredients for dishes such as fried rice and Chow Mein (page 77).

Cha Shao Roast Pork (top); Braised Spare Ribs in Brown Sauce (bottom).

Barbecue Pork Spare-Ribs.

Barbecue Pork Spare-Ribs

Most pork spare-ribs contain a great deal of fat which causes the barbecue to flame during cooking, so you often end up with a pile of charred ribs that are underdone inside. One way of avoiding this is to precook the spare-ribs in a marinade, then crisp them on the barbecue to acquire that slightly charred look.

1 kg (2¼ lb) pork spare-ribs
275 ml (½ pint) water

Marinade:
2 cloves garlic, crushed
2 slices peeled fresh root ringer, crushed
3 tablespoons crushed yellow bean paste, or
* 3 tablespoons soy sauce with 1 tablespoon cornflour*
1 tablespoon sugar
1 tablespoon vinegar
2-3 tablespoons Shao Hsing rice wine or dry sherry
1 teaspoon chilli sauce
1 teaspoon sesame seed oil

Trim the excess fat and gristle from the meat, then cut into individual ribs. Mix together the marinade ingredients in a large bowl or dish. Add the spare-ribs, cover and marinate for 4-6 hours, turning several times.

Place the spare-ribs in a wok or large pot with the water and bring to the boil, then reduce the heat and cook gently for 20-25 minutes. Remove the ribs from the liquid to cool for a little, discarding the liquid.

Barbecue the ribs on a hot grid for about 10 minutes, turning them frequently, and basting with the sauce. Serve hot.

Five-Spice Pork Spare-Ribs

Ideally, chop each individual rib into 2 or 3 bite-size pieces before cooking so you can put a whole piece into your mouth; chew it by biting the meat on either side of the bone. This is far less messy than gnawing at a whole rib like a dog with a bone.

1 kg (2¼ lb) pork spare-ribs

Marinade:
1 teaspoon salt
1 tablespoon sugar
1 tablespoon light soy sauce
2 tablespoons dark soy sauce
3 tablespoons Shao Hsing rice wine or dry sherry
1 teaspoon five-spice powder
2 teaspoons curry powder
2 tablespoons Hoi Sin sauce or barbecue sauce

Trim the excess fat and gristle from the spare-ribs and chop each rib into 2 or 3 small pieces. Mix together the marinade ingredients in a baking tin. Add the spare-ribs, cover and marinate for 4-6 hours, turning several times.

Preheat the oven to 230C/450F/Gas 8 for 15 minutes, then reduce the oven to 200C/400F/Gas 6 and cook for another 20-25 minutes, turning once or twice.

Note: Overcooking will render the meat too dry and flaky or tough, instead of being tender and succulent. When correctly done, the meat comes off the bones easily.

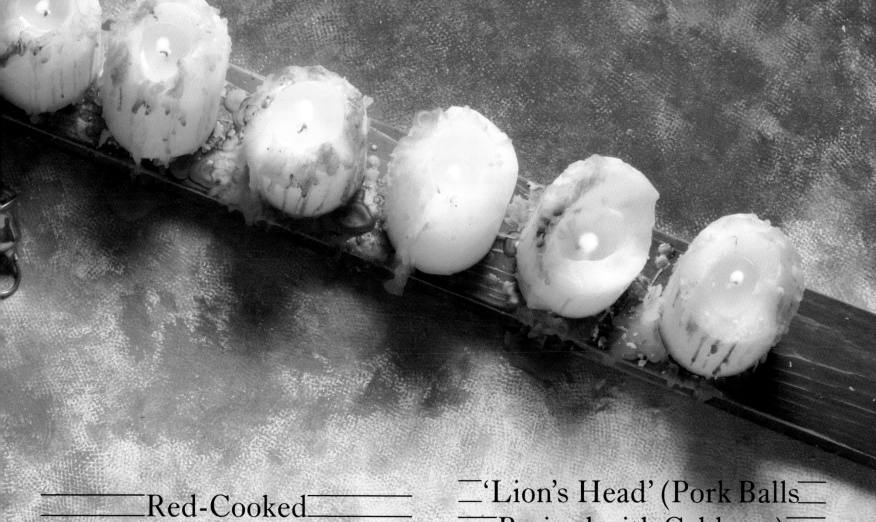

Red-Cooked Pork Shoulder

In China, particularly south of the Yangtze River, this dish is a must for any feast or festivities, big or small; it is the nearest equivalent to a traditional Sunday joint in the West.

1.6-1.8 kg (3½-4 lb) pork shoulder with rind
4-5 spring onions
3-4 slices fresh peeled root ginger
6 tablespoons dark soy sauce
4-5 tablespoons Shao Hsing rice wine or brandy
100 g (4 oz) rock candy or crystallized sugar

To garnish:
500 g (1 lb) spinach or cabbage leaves
2 tablespoons oil
½ teaspoon salt

Clean the pork, removing all the bristles in the rind with tweezers, then scraping it with a sharp knife. Pat dry with kitchen paper. Crush the spring onions and ginger with the flat blade of a cleaver or heavy knife.

Blanch the pork by placing it in a pot of boiling water for a few minutes, then discard the water and rinse the meat under cold running water. Place a bamboo rack or 2 pairs of bamboo chopsticks criss-cross on the bottom of a large saucepan or pot to prevent the meat from sticking to the pan and burning. Place the pork in the pan, rind-side down, score the meat with a few cuts, add all the seasonings and enough cold water to cover. Bring to the boil over high heat and skim off the scum. Reduce the heat to low, and simmer, covered, for about 2 hours.

To serve, remove the pork to a serving dish. Reduce and thicken the sauce by cooking it over high heat, uncovered. Pour it over the meat. Meanwhile, stir-fry the spinach or cabbage in hot oil with salt, then place around the pork as a garnish.

'Lion's Head' (Pork Balls Braised with Cabbage)

This dish is so-called because the meat balls are supposed to resemble the shape of a lion's head, and the cabbage is supposed to look like its mane. Again, this is another great favourite of mine, and indeed of all the children (of all ages) in China.

500 g (1 lb) lean pork, coarsely minced
100 g (4 oz) fatty pork, coarsely minced
225 g (8 oz) crab meat, coarsely chopped
2 spring onions, finely chopped
1 teaspoon finely chopped peeled fresh root ginger
2-3 tablespoons Shao Hsing rice wine or dry sherry
2 teaspoons sugar
2 tablespoons light soy sauce
1 tablespoon cornflour
1 teaspoon salt
500 g (1 lb) Chinese cabbage
3 tablespoons oil
275 ml (½ pint) chicken stock

Mix together the minced pork with crab meat, spring onions, ginger, wine, sugar, soy sauce, cornflour and half the salt. Blend well and shape the mixture into 4-6 large round balls.

Cut the cabbage in quarters lengthwise. Heat the oil in a large saucepan or casserole and stir-fry the cabbage when the oil is hot. Add the remaining salt and continue stirring until the cabbage quarters are covered with oil, then place the meatballs on the cabbage. Pour the chicken stock over the top and bring to the boil, then cover tightly, reduce the heat and simmer gently for 25-30 minutes. Serve hot.

Alternatively, you can brown the meatballs in a little hot oil before placing them on top of the cabbage and cooking in the oven in a casserole at 180C/350F/Gas 4. You can serve it directly from the casserole, or if cooked in a saucepan, transfer the cabbage to a large bowl with the meatballs arranged on top.

Steamed Pork in Ground Rice

This used to be one of my favourite dishes when I was a child, perhaps because it was always eaten as a festival food to mark the coming of summer (usually early in May in southern China). This dish is so delicious that children in China eat mounds of it; as a joke, they are weighed before and after the meal to see how much weight they have put on in the process.

700 g (1½ lb) boneless pork shoulder with rind
3-4 tablespoons light soy sauce
2 tablespoons Shao Hsing rice wine or dry sherry
2 teaspoons sugar
100 g (4 oz) uncooked rice
1 star anise or ½ teaspoon five-spice powder

Cut the pork into 5×7 cm (2×3 inch) thin slices, then marinate with the soy sauce, wine and sugar for 25-30 minutes.

Put the rice and star anise or five-spice powder in a wok or frying-pan and stir over a high heat for about 30 seconds, then reduce heat to low and continue stirring until golden brown. Remove and crush with a rolling pin into coarse bits.

Coat each slice of pork with the ground rice, pressing it in well, then arrange the pork, piece by piece, in a large heatproof bowl or pudding basin, skin-side down. Steam vigorously for at least 3 hours or until the meat is very tender.

To serve, turn the bowl or basin upside down on a dish so that when the bowl is removed, the meat slices will remain on the dish with the skin-side up.

Red-Cooked Beef with Tomatoes.

Red-Cooked Beef with Tomatoes

This recipe is from Tianjin in northern China. Shin of beef would be ideal for this dish.

700 g (1½ lb) stewing or braising beef
2-3 spring onions, cut into short lengths
2-3 slices peeled fresh root ginger, crushed
450 g (1 lb) tomatoes
75 g (3 oz) sugar
2 tablespoons oil
2 cloves garlic, crushed
2-3 tablespoons Shao Hsing rice wine or dry sherry
2 tablespoons light soy sauce
1 tablespoon dark soy sauce
2 teaspoons cornflour mixed with a little water to a smooth paste
salt and pepper

Place the beef, in large pieces, in a saucepan and cover with cold water. Add half the spring onions and ginger and bring to the boil, then reduce the heat and simmer tightly covered for about 1 hour.

Skin the tomatoes by quickly plunging them in boiling water, then cut them into small pieces. Stew them with about half the sugar in a small saucepan until they become a pulp.

Remove the beef from the cooking liquid, reserving the liquid. Cool the beef a little before cubing.

Meanwhile, heat the oil in a preheated wok or large frying pan. Add the crushed garlic, remaining spring onions and ginger to flavour the oil, then add the beef. Stir for about 1 minute or until lightly golden. Add the wine, soy sauce, remaining sugar and the tomatoes and about 275 ml (½ pint) cooking liquid. Bring to the boil, blend well and cook for about 5 minutes or until most of the liquid is reduced. Thicken the sauce with the cornflour mixture. Adjust the seasonings and serve hot.

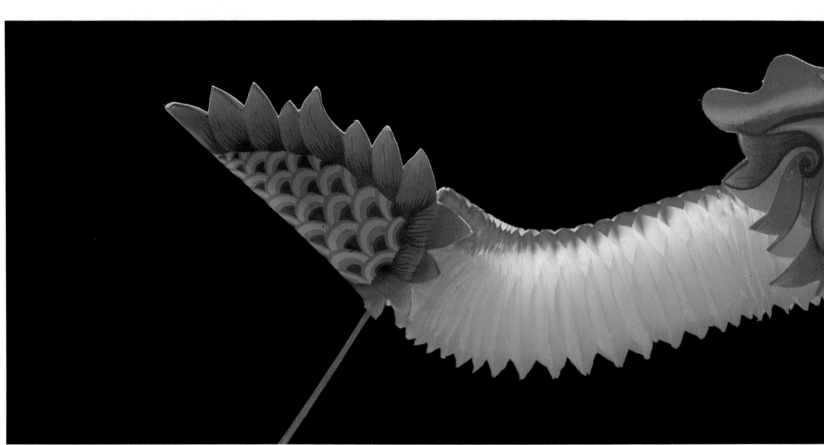

Long-Braised Brisket of Beef

To a Chinese palate, beef always tastes a trifle strong and tough, that is why the cheaper cuts of beef are often cooked for a long time by long-braising with plenty of seasonings and spices.

1 kg (2¼ lb) brisket of beef
850 ml (1½ pints) water
2 tablespoons sugar
2-3 tablespoons oil
3 slices peeled fresh root ginger, crushed
3 spring onions, cut into short lengths
2 tablespoons light soy sauce
3 tablespoons dark soy sauce
3-4 tablespoons Shao Hsing rice wine or brandy
1 teaspoon five-spice powder
1 tablespoon cornflour mixed with a little water to a smooth paste

Trim any excess fat from the beef, but remember that the sinew helps to enrich the juice and keep the meat tender. Cut the beef into 2.5 cm (1 inch) cubes, or slightly longer chunks of the same width.

Bring the water to the boil and parboil the beef rapidly for about 3 minutes. Turn off the heat and remove the beef. Add about 1 tablespoon sugar to the water and set aside; after about 10 minutes all the impurities will sink to the bottom of the pan, leaving the stock clear. Drain through a fine sieve and reserve.

Heat the oil in a preheated wok or frying-pan. Add the ginger and spring onions to flavour the oil, then stir-fry the beef for about 1 minute. Add the soy sauce, wine, sugar and five-spice powder and continue stirring for another minute or so, then transfer to a saucepan or pot and add the stock. Bring to the boil over high heat, cover tightly, reduce the heat to low and simmer gently for 2 hours; the juices should be reduced to not much more than 275 ml (½ pint), and have become a rich, brown sauce with a wonderful aroma.

Add the cornflour mixture to the beef, increase the heat to high and stir to thicken the sauce. Serve hot.

Stewed Five-Spice Beef or Mutton

This is a very simple way of cooking the cheaper cuts of beef or mutton – or indeed any type of meat, such as veal or lamb. It can be cooked the day before, then warmed and served whenever you wish.

1 kg (2¼ lb) stewing beef, mutton or lamb
1 litre (1¾ pints) water
2-3 spring onions, cut into short lengths
2-3 slices peeled fresh root ginger
1 teaspoon five-spice powder
3 tablespoons Shao Hsing rice wine or brandy
1 teaspoon salt
50 g (2 oz) rock candy or crystallized sugar
2-3 tablespoons soy sauce
225 g (8 oz) carrots, potatoes or Chinese radishes

Cut the meat into cubes, then soak them in water for 30 minutes. Rinse and drain well on kitchen paper.

Bring the water to the boil in a saucepan or pot and add the meat. When the water returns to the boil, skim the surface, then add spring onions, ginger, five-spice powder, wine and salt. Reduce the heat and simmer gently, covered, for 1 hour. Add the sugar and soy sauce and increase the heat to reduce and thicken the sauce. Cut the carrots or potato into small cubes and add to the stew about 25-30 minutes before serving.

Vegetarian Casserole

As explained earlier, the Chinese never mix different
ingredients indiscriminately; these items are carefully
selected to achieve an harmonious balance of colour, aroma,
flavour and texture.

15 g (½ oz) wood ears
1 cake bean curd (tofu)
100 g (4 oz) French beans or mange-tout
100 g (4 oz) broccoli or Chinese cabbage
100 g (4 oz) bamboo shoots or baby corn
100 g (4 oz) carrots
3-4 tablespoons oil
1 teaspoon salt
1 teaspoon sugar
1 tablespoon light soy sauce
1 teaspoon cornflour mixed with a little water to make a smooth paste
1 teaspoon sesame seed oil

Soak the wood ears in water for 20-25 minutes. Rinse well and discard
the hard bits, if any. Cut the bean curd into about 12 small pieces,
then harden them in a pot of lightly salted boiling water for 2-3
minutes. Remove and drain well.

Top and tail the French beans or mange-tout. Cut the remaining
vegetables into thin slices or chunks.

Heat about half of the oil in a flameproof casserole or saucepan
until hot and lightly brown the bean curd pieces on all sides. Remove
with a slotted spoon and set aside.

Heat the remaining oil and stir-fry the remaining vegetables for
about 1 minute, then add the bean curd, salt, sugar and soy sauce and
continue stirring to blend well. Add a little stock or water and bring to
the boil, then reduce the heat and simmer gently, covered, for about 2
minutes.

Pour the cornflour mixture over the vegetables and stir, increas-
ing the heat to thicken the sauce. Add the sesame seed oil to garnish.
Serve hot.

Vegetarian Casserole.

Steamed Chicken with Chinese Mushrooms

This is a Cantonese recipe; the best result is achieved by using the breasts and thighs of a very young chicken.

700 g (1½ lb) chicken breasts and/or thighs
1 tablespoon light soy sauce
1 tablespoon Shao Hsing rice wine or dry sherry
1 teaspoon sugar
2 teaspoons cornflour
3-4 dried Chinese mushrooms, soaked
2 slices peeled fresh root ginger, thinly shredded
1 teaspoon sesame seed oil
salt
ground Sichuan pepper

Chop the chicken through the bone into small bite-size pieces. Mix together the soy sauce, wine, sugar and cornflour, then marinate the chicken in the mixture for 25-30 minutes. Squeeze dry the soaked mushrooms, discarding hard stalks. Thinly shred the mushrooms.

Place the chicken pieces on a heatproof plate and arrange the mushrooms and ginger on top. Garnish with sesame seed oil and salt and pepper. Place the plate on the rack inside a hot steamer and cook vigorously for only 20 minutes. Serve hot.

Cantonese Chicken

This is the bright brown chicken seen hanging in the windows of some Cantonese restaurants.

1 roasting chicken, about 1.7 kg (3½ lb)
1 teaspoon salt
1 tablespoon oil
1 teaspoon finely chopped peeled fresh root ginger
2 spring onions, finely chopped
1 tablespoon sugar
1 tablespoon Hoi Sin sauce
2 tablespoons Shao Hsing rice wine or dry sherry
2 teaspoons five-spice powder
2 tablespoons honey dissolved in 125 ml (4 fl oz) water
2 tablespoons dark soy sauce
1 tablespoon sesame seed oil

Clean the chicken well and pat dry inside and out, then rub inside and out with salt. Tie the neck opening tightly with string so that no liquid will drip out when hanging upside-down.

Heat the oil in a saucepan over moderate heat. Add the ginger, spring onions, sugar, Hoi Sin sauce, wine and five-spice powder. Bring to the boil, stirring constantly, then pour the liquid into the cavity of the chicken and securely sew up.

Plunge the whole chicken into a large pot of boiling water for a few seconds only. Remove and brush thoroughly first with the honey, then soy sauce. Hang up to dry for at least 5 hours.

Roast the chicken in a 200C/400F/Gas 6 oven, hanging on a meat hook with its head down; place a tray of cold water in the bottom of the oven to catch the drips. After about 25 minutes reduce the heat to 180C/350F/Gas 4, and roast for a further 30 minutes, basting once or twice with the remaining honey and soy sauce. Remove from the oven and brush with sesame seed oil, then cool. Remove the strings and pour the liquid out into a bowl or jug to use as a sauce to pour over the chicken after it has been chopped into small bite-sized pieces (page 7). Serve hot or cold.

Drunken Chicken

Also known as 'Imperial Concubine Chicken', partly because the concubine referred to here is the Empress Yang Kwei-fei of the Tang dynasty, noted for her beauty, as well as her fondness for alcohol. You may find this dish very similar in flavour to a Coq au Vin.

1 young chicken, about 1.4 kg (3 lb)
2 tablespoons light soy sauce
2 tablespoons Shao Hsing rice wine or dry sherry
1 litre (1¾ pints) oil for deep frying
1 teaspoon salt
1 teaspoon crushed Sichuan peppercorns
2 slices peeled fresh root ginger
2 spring onions, cut into short lengths
3-4 tablespoons dark soy sauce
175 ml (6 fl oz) Chinese red wine or tawny port

Clean and dry the chicken well. Mix together the light soy sauce and wine and pour over the bird, inside and out, and marinate for 25-30 minutes.

Heat the oil in a wok or deep-fat fryer until hot. Deep-fry the chicken until lightly brown all over, then remove and immerse in a Chinese sand-pot or flame-proof casserole of boiling water. Add the salt, pepper, ginger, spring onions, dark soy sauce and red wine or port. Return to the boil, then reduce the heat and simmer gently, covered, for at least 1½ hours, turning once or twice.

Serve either in a large bowl or in the casserole. The chicken should be so tender that it falls to pieces with a pair of chopsticks.

Red-Cooked Chicken

This is probably the most popular method of cooking a chicken in China. The main feature of this dish is that it provides plenty of rich sauce, to which vegetables, such as bamboo shoots, mushrooms or carrots, can be added to absorb the savouriness, as well as to harmonize the flavours.

1 young chicken, about 1.4 kg (3 lb)
2-3 tablespoons oil
3 slices peeled fresh root ginger, chopped into small pieces
2-3 spring onions, cut into short lengths
1 teaspoon salt
1 tablespoon sugar
2 tablespoons Shao Hsing rice wine or dry sherry
3 tablespoons dark soy sauce
275 g (½ pint) stock (page 24) or water

Joint the chicken, then chop it through the bone into 20-24 bite-sized pieces with skin attached (page 7).

Heat the oil in a preheated wok or saucepan until smoking. Add the ginger and spring onions to flavour the oil for a few seconds, then quickly add the chicken pieces and stir-fry for about 2-3 minutes or until lightly browned. Add the salt, sugar, wine and soy sauce, stirring until well blended, then add the stock or water and bring to the boil, stirring constantly. Reduce the heat to moderate and braise, covered, for 20-25 minutes, stirring occasionally so the chicken pieces do not stick to the bottom of the wok or pan. Just before serving, uncover and increase the heat to high again. Stir and cook for about 5 minutes to reduce and thicken the sauce. Alternatively, you can add about 500 g (1 lb) vegetables, cut into small pieces, to the chicken and cook for 10-15 minutes before serving.

Long-Braised Chicken in Brown Sauce

Chicken legs, thighs and drumsticks are ideal for this dish – chicken breast meat is best for quick-fried dishes.

4 chicken legs (or 4 thighs and 4 drumsticks)
½ teaspoon salt
1 tablespoon sugar
1 tablespoon dark soy sauce
2 tablespoons Shao Hsing rice wine or dry sherry
2 teaspoons cornflour
600 ml (1 pint) oil for deep-frying
2 cloves garlic, crushed
2-3 spring onions, cut into short lengths with white and green parts separated
2 dried red chillies, seeded and cut into small pieces
2 tablespoons crushed yellow bean paste
275 ml (½ pint) stock (page 24) or water

Chop each thigh and drumstick through the bone into 3-4 bite-sized pieces. Marinate with the salt, sugar, soy sauce, wine and cornflour for 15-20 minutes, stirring once or twice.

Heat the oil in a wok or deep-fat fryer until hot. Deep-fry the chicken pieces for 1-2 minutes, stirring to separate, then remove and drain well on kitchen paper.

Pour off excess oil, leaving about 1 tablespoon in the wok. Add the garlic, spring onions (white parts only at this stage), chillies and the bean paste, stirring for 25-30 seconds. Add the chicken pieces, blending well, then add about one-third of the stock or water and bring to the boil. Cook over high heat for 5 minutes, stirring gently to make sure the chicken pieces do not stick to the bottom of the wok or pan. Add a little more stock or water and cook for about 5 minutes more, stirring. Add the green parts of the spring onions and the remaining stock or water, then braise for 5 minutes more or until the sauce is almost entirely absorbed. Serve hot.

Hunan Chicken in Spicy Sauce

Also known as 'Dong An Chicken'. *Dong An*, 'East Peace' in Chinese, is a small town in Hunan where this very popular dish originated.

1 young chicken, about 1 kg (2¼ lb)
3-4 dried Chinese mushrooms, soaked
3-4 dried red chillies
2 slices peeled fresh root ginger
2 spring onions
1 teaspoon Sichuan peppercorns
3 tablespoons oil
1 teaspoon salt
1 tablespoon soy sauce
1 tablespoon vinegar
2 tablespoons Shao Hsing rice wine or brandy
125 ml (4 fl oz) stock (page 24) or water
2 teaspoons cornflour mixed with 1 tablespoon water
1 teaspoon sesame seed oil

Clean the chicken inside and out, then plunge into a pot of boiling water for 10 minutes. Remove and rinse in cold water, then leave to cool for about 1 hour before taking the meat off the bone (but keep the skin on). Cut the chicken meat into long, thin strips.

Squeeze the mushrooms dry, discarding the hard stalks. Thinly shred the mushrooms, ginger and spring onions and crush the peppercorns.

Heat the oil in a preheated work or pan, then add the chillies, ginger, spring onions and peppercorns to flavour the oil. Add the chicken and mushrooms and stir for a few seconds, then add salt, soy sauce, vinegar and wine, stirring to blend. Add the stock or water and braise over high heat until the sauce is reduced to almost nothing. Finally, add the cornflour and water mixture, blending well until thickened. Add the sesame seed oil and serve hot.

Crispy Deep-Fried Chicken

Traditionally, a whole chicken is jointed into eight pieces – two wings, breasts, thighs and drumsticks – for this dish. But you can use just one part of chicken, such as 12 drumsticks or wings.

12 chicken joints
1 teaspoon salt
1 teaspoon sugar
2-3 tablespoons Shao Hsing rice wine or dry sherry
2 tablespoons soy sauce
1 teaspoon five-spice powder, or curry powder
275 ml (½ pint) stock or water
2-3 tablespoons plain flour or fresh breadcrumbs
1 litre (1¾ pints) oil for deep-frying
2 tablespoons Hoi Sin sauce or barbecue sauce (optional)

Marinate the chicken pieces in the salt, sugar, wine, soy sauce and five-spice or curry powder for at least 30 minutes, turning occasionally to make sure they are all covered.

Bring the stock or water to the boil, add the chicken pieces with the marinade and gently simmer for 15 minutes. Turn off the heat and leave the chicken to cool in the sauce for 2-3 hours, then remove and drain well on kitchen paper, reserving the sauce.

Heat the oil in a wok or deep-fat fryer until hot. Coat each chicken piece with flour or breadcrumbs. Reduce the heat and deep-fry the chicken for about 5 minutes or until golden all over, then remove and drain well on kitchen paper. Increase the heat to high again and wait for the oil to get hot once more, then return the chicken pieces to crisp until golden brown all over. Remove and drain well.

Blend the sauce with Hoi Sin sauce or barbecue sauce until smooth (a dash of chilli sauce can be added, if liked). Serve hot or cold as a dipping sauce with the chicken pieces.

Hunan Chicken in Spicy Sauce (left); Crispy Deep-Fried Chicken (right).

Long-Simmered Duck

Long-simmering is a very simple method of cooking. There are two kinds of long-simmered dishes. The first is like a soup, in which very few supplementary ingredients, or none at all, are used, and the seasoning is not added until just before the completion of cooking. It is particularly suitable for food like chicken and pork. Stronger flavoured food, such as duck and beef, are more suited for the second kind of long-simmering, which is more like a stew, as in this recipe.

1 duckling, about 1.8 kg (4 lb), or 2 duck breasts, 2 legs and thighs, about 1 kg (2¼ lb) in total
2-3 slices peeled fresh root ginger
2-3 spring onions
4 tablespoons soy sauce
4 tablespoons Shao Hsing rice wine or dry sherry
50 g (2 oz) rock candy or crystal sugar
1 teaspoon five-spice powder
6-8 dried Chinese mushrooms, soaked
2-3 carrots
700 g (1½ lb) Chinese cabbage

If using a whole duck, quarter it by chopping through the bone into four pieces – 2 breasts and two legs. Plunge the pieces into a pot of boiling water and rapidly boil for 4-5 minutes, then discard about two-thirds of the water. Add the ginger, spring onions, soy sauce, wine, sugar and five-spice powder. Return to the boil again, then reduce the heat and simmer gently, covered, for 1½ hours.

Meanwhile, squeeze dry the mushrooms, discarding the hard stalks. Cut the carrots into small slices and the cabbage into large chunks, then add the vegetables to the duck. Increase the heat and cook for 15-20 minutes. Serve hot, adjusting seasonings if necessary.

Aromatic Crispy Duck

Because this dish is on the menu of most Peking-style restaurants, it is often confused with the world-renowned Peking Duck. This duck dish, in fact, originated in Shandong, where the same method is often used for cooking a chicken.

1 duckling, about 1.8 kg (4 lb)
2 teaspoons salt
5 star anise or 1 teaspoon five-spice powder
1 tablespoon Sichuan peppercorns
1 teaspoon cloves
3 cinnamon sticks
2-3 spring onions
4 slices unpeeled fresh root ginger
4-5 tablespoons Shao Hsing rice wine or dry sherry
5 tablespoons soy sauce
1 litre (1¾ pints) oil for deep-frying
leaves of 1 head lettuce and salt and ground Sichuan pepper, to serve

Clean the duck well, then cut off the wings and split in half down the backbone; rub with salt on both sides. Marinate in a deep dish with the remaining ingredients, except the oil, for at least 3-4 hours, turning several times.

Steam the duck with marinade vigorously for 2-3 hours, then remove from cooking liquid and leave to cool for at least 5 hours. (Unless the skin is cold and dry, the duck will not be crispy.)

Heat the oil in a wok or deep fat fryer until smoking. Place the duck halves in the oil, skin-side down, and fry for 8-10 minutes or until crispy and brown, turning once or twice. Remove and drain well on kitchen paper. As soon as the duck is cool enough to handle, chop into small bite-size pieces, and serve on a bed of lettuce leaves with tiny bowls of salt and pepper into which the duck can be dipped. Alternatively, pull the meat off the bone, and serve it with spring onions and duck sauce wrapped in lettuce leaves or pancakes like the Peking Duck (see picture on page 43).

Peking Duck

What makes this dish so unique is not so much the way it is cooked, but the specially-reared species of duck used. The original recipe runs into several thousand words, starting with a detailed description of how to make up the duck feed, continuing with complicated instructions on how to build and fire the oven. Here is a simplified version for cooking in a Western kitchen, using a fresh Aylesbury duck. Remember the skin of the duck must be absolutely dry before cooking – the drier the skin, the crispier the duck.

1 oven-ready duckling, about 2.3 kg (5 lb)
2 tablespoons honey dissolved in 275 ml (½ pint) warm water and 1 tablespoon vinegar

Sauce:
1 tablespoon sesame seed oil
8 tablespoons crushed yellow bean paste
2 tablespoons sugar

To serve:
24 thin pancakes (page 77)
1 medium cucumber
1 bunch spring onions

Clean the duck well, then cut off the wings. Plunge the bird in a pot of boiling water for 2-3 minutes to seal the pores, making the skin airtight and preventing the fat from escaping during roasting. Brush the duck all over with the honey and vinegar solution while the skin is still hot, then hang it up to dry in a cool and well ventilated spot for at least 4 hours; use a fan heater or even a hairdryer if in a hurry.

Preheat the oven to 200C/400F/Gas 6. Place the duck, breast side up, on a wire rack in a roasting pan, and roast for 1½-1¾ hours without basting or turning.

Meanwhile, make the pancakes (page 77). Make the sauce by mixing the sugar and sesame seed oil with the yellow bean paste over low heat for 2-3 minutes, stirring constantly, until smooth. Cut the cucumber into thin strips the size of matchsticks and thinly shred the spring onions.

To serve, the crispy skin of the duck is peeled off in small slices with a sharp carving knife, then the juicy meat is carved and served on a separate dish.

To eat, spread 1 teaspoon of the sauce over a pancake, place a few strips of cucumber and spring onions in the centre and place 1-2 slices of crispy skin and 2-3 slices of duck meat on top, then roll up the pancake, tucking in the ends to prevent the sauce from oozing out. Eat with your fingers like a sausage roll.

The carcass of the duck is traditionally made into a delicious soup and served with Chinese cabbage with seasonings at the end of the meal (page 26).

Note: Hoi Sin sauce, also known as barbecue sauce, can be used instead of making your own sauce. Also, ready-made pancakes are available in most Chinese supermarkets, or use the Greek pitta bread as a substitute.

Mixed Meat Casserole

One of the outstanding characteristics of Chinese cuisine is the way various meats, seafood, vegetables and other ingredients are combined to make a dish that is harmonious in flavour, texture and visual appeal. This recipe from Canton is a typical example.

4 dried Chinese mushrooms, soaked
225 g (8 oz) Chinese cabbage or lettuce leaves
2 cakes bean curd (tofu), cut into small cubes
100 g (4 oz) Cha Shao Roast Pork (page 33), or Chinese sausage, thinly sliced
100 g (4 oz) Crispy Roast Pork (page 30), or any other cooked meat, thinly sliced
100 g (4 oz) cooked chicken or duck, boned and sliced
100 g (4 oz) peeled prawns
100 g (4 oz) cooked ham, cut into small cubes
1 teaspoon salt
2-3 tablespoons Shao Hsing rice wine or dry sherry
2 tablespoons light soy sauce
275 ml (½ pint) stock (page 24)
2 spring onions, cut into short lengths, to garnish

Squeeze dry the mushrooms, discarding the stalks. Depending on their size, cut them in half or quarters.

Line a casserole or Chinese sand-pot with the cabbage or lettuce leaves. Add the bean curd, place the cooked meats on top with seasonings and stock. Bring to the boil and simmer gently, covered, for 30 minutes. Add the spring onions to garnish. Serve hot straight from the casserole.

Peking Duck.

Cantonese Steamed Fish in Black Bean Sauce

If you do not possess a wok or a steamer big enough to take a whole fish, it is possible to bake the fish in a 200C/400F/Gas 6 oven for 20-30 minutes, turning and basting once.

1 sea bass, trout, grey mullet, sole or turbot, about 700g (1½ lb)
½ teaspoon salt
1 teaspoon sesame seed oil
2-3 spring onions, cut in half lengthways
1 tablespoon salted black beans
1 tablespoon light soy sauce
2 tablespoons Shao Hsing rice wine or dry sherry
1 teaspoon finely chopped peeled fresh root ginger
2 tablespoons vegetable oil
2 spring onions, finely shredded

Scale, gut and clean the fish if necessary. Dry thoroughly, then score both sides of the fish as deep as the bone at 1.5 cm (¾ inch) intervals (this is not necessary for a flat fish). Rub the inside of the fish with salt and sesame seed oil, then place on top of the spring onions on a heat-proof platter.

Crush the black beans and blend together with the soy sauce, wine and ginger, then pour evenly all over the fish. Place the fish in a hot steamer or inside a wok on a rack, and steam vigorously for 15 minutes or until cooked through.

To serve, heat the oil until hot, place the shredded spring onions on top of the fish, then pour the oil over the whole length of the fish. Serve immediately.

Crab with Spring Onions and Ginger

This is a Cantonese recipe that is interchangeable with the Lobster in Black Bean Sauce (page 46). This is best eaten with your fingers, so have ready finger bowls and paper napkins.

1 large or 2 medium crabs, weighing about 1 kg (2 lb) in total
2 tablespoons Shao Hsing rice wine or dry sherry
1 egg, lightly beaten
1 tablespoon cornflour
3-4 tablespoons oil
1 clove garlic, crushed
1 tablespoon finely chopped peeled fresh root ginger
3-4 spring onions, finely chopped
2 tablespoons soy sauce
2 teaspoons sugar
75 ml (3 fl oz) stock (page 24) or water

Break off the legs and claws of the crabs, then crack them with the back of a Chinese cleaver or heavy knife; crack the shell and break it into several pieces, discarding the feathery gills and the sac. Marinate the crab pieces with wine, egg and cornflour for 10-15 minutes.

Heat the oil in a preheated wok or frying pan until smoking. Flavour the oil with garlic for a few seconds, then remove and discard. Stir-fry the crab pieces for about 1 minute, then add the ginger, spring onions, soy sauce and sugar, blending well. Add the stock or water and bring to the boil, braising the crab for 3-4 minutes, stirring constantly. As soon as the sauce is reduced to almost nothing, serve immediately.

Sichuan Braised Fish in Hot Bean Sauce

This is the Sichuan version of Red-Cooked Fish (page 46). The method is almost the same, but with a quite distinctive flavour.

1 carp, sea bass, trout or grey mullet, about 700g (1½ lb)
600 ml (1 pint) oil for deep-frying
1 clove garlic, finely chopped
1 teaspoon finely chopped peeled fresh root ginger
2-3 spring onions, finely chopped with the white and green parts separated
1 tablespoon chilli bean sauce
1 tablespoon tomato purée
1 tablespoon soy sauce
1 teaspoon salt
2 teaspoons sugar
2 tablespoons Shao Hsing rice wine or dry sherry
225 ml (8 fl oz) stock (page 24) or water
1 tablespoon vinegar
1 tablespoon cornflour mixed with a little water

Scale, gut and clean the fish, if necessary. Dry thoroughly, then diagonally slash both sides as deep as the bone at 1 cm (½ in) intervals.

Heat the oil in a wok or deep-fat fryer until smoking. Deep-fry the fish until golden on both sides, then remove and drain well on kitchen paper.

Pour off the excess oil, leaving about 1 tablespoon in the wok. Add the garlic, ginger, the white parts of the spring onions, chilli bean paste, tomato purée, soy sauce, salt, sugar, wine and stock or water. Bring to the boil, then return the fish to the wok, reduce the heat and simmer gently for 3-4 minutes, turning the fish over two or three

Scale, gut and clean the fish, if necessary. Dry thoroughly and score both sides with several cuts as far as the bone. Rub with salt both inside and out. Marinate in wine for a few minutes, then coat the fish with beaten egg and cornflour.

Heat the oil in a wok or deep-fat fryer until almost boiling. Lower the fish in and deep-fry for 5-6 minutes or until golden and crisp all round. Remove with a slotted spoon or strainer and place on a warm serving platter.

Pour off the excess oil, leaving about 2 tablespoons in the wok. Squeeze the mushrooms dry, discarding the hard stalks, then dice. Add the diced mushrooms, bamboo shoots, carrot, prawns, peas, ginger and spring onions and stir-fry for 1 minute. Add the soy sauce, sugar, vinegar, tomato purée and stock or water, then bring to the boil, stirring constantly. Thicken the sauce with the cornflour and water mixture, then pour the sauce all over the fish. Serve hot.

Steamed Whole Fish with 'White' Sauce

This recipe comes from Hubei in central China. Known as The Province of a Thousand Lakes, as well as The Land of Fish and Rice, one of its specialities is fish cookery.

*1 bream, carp, trout, sea bass, sole, grey mullet, grouper or
  sea bream, weighing about 700 g (1½ lb)*
1 teaspoon salt
2 tablespoons Shao Hsing rice wine or dry sherry
2-3 spring onions
2-3 slices peeled fresh root ginger

Sauce:
2-3 dried Chinese mushrooms, soaked
25 g (1 oz) cooked ham
25 g (1 oz) bamboo shoots
50 g (2 oz) peeled prawns, defrosted if frozen
25 g (1 oz) peas
2 tablespoons oil
1-2 spring onions, finely chopped
1 teaspoon finely chopped peeled fresh root ginger
1 teaspoon salt
125 ml (4 fl oz) stock (page 24)
2 teaspoons cornflour mixed with 1 tablespoon milk

Scale, gut and clean the fish, if necessary. Dry thoroughly, then score both sides of the fish as deep as the bone at 1 cm (½ inch) intervals. Rub the salt inside and out, then marinate with the wine for 3 minutes.

Place the fish on top of half of the spring onions and ginger on a heatproof dish, and place the remaining spring onions and ginger on top. Steam vigorously in a hot steamer for approximately 15 minutes or until cooked through.

Meanwhile, squeeze the mushrooms dry and discard the hard stalks. Dice the mushrooms, bamboo shoots and ham into pieces about the same size as the prawns and peas.

Heat the oil in a wok or frying pan until hot, add the finely chopped spring onions, ginger, diced mushrooms, ham, bamboo shoots and prawns and peas. Stir-fry for about 1 minute, then add the salt and stock, bringing to the boil. Reduce the heat and thicken the sauce with the cornflour and milk mixture. Place the cooked fish on a serving platter and pour the sauce over. Serve immediately.

times. Carefully lift the fish on to a serving platter. Increase the heat to high again, add the vinegar and the green part of the spring onions to the sauce and thicken with the cornflour and water mixture, stirring until smooth, then pour it over the fish. Serve immediately.

Braised Fish in Sweet and Sour Sauce

This is a slightly simplified version of the famous 'Squirrel' fish from eastern China.

1 carp, bream, sea bass, grouper or grey mullet, about 700 g (1½ lb)
1 teaspoon salt
1 tablespoon Shao Hsing rice wine or dry sherry
1 egg, lightly beaten
2-3 tablespoons cornflour
600 ml (1 pint) oil for deep-frying

Sauce:
3-4 dried Chinese mushrooms, soaked
50 g (2 oz) bamboo shoots, diced
50 g (2 oz) carrot, diced
50 g (2 oz) peeled prawns, defrosted if frozen
50 g (2 oz) green peas
1 teaspoon finely chopped peeled fresh root ginger
2 spring onions, finely chopped
1 tablespoon soy sauce
2 tablespoons sugar
2 tablespoons vinegar
1 tablespoon tomato purée
125 ml (4 fl oz) stock (page 24) or water
2 teaspoons cornflour mixed with 1 tablespoon cold water

Red-Cooked Fish

In China, a fish weighing less than 1 kg (2¼ lb) is often cooked whole, with its head and tail intact. The fish is scored on both sides to allow the heat to penetrate more quickly, and at the same time help to diffuse the flavour of the seasonings.

1 carp, sea bass, grey mullet or trout, about 700g (1½ lb)
3-4 tablespoons oil
2-3 slices peeled fresh root ginger, thinly shredded
2-3 spring onions, thinly shredded
1 teaspoon salt
1 teaspoon sugar
1 tablespoon soy sauce
1-2 tablespoons Shao Hsing rice wine or dry sherry
275 ml (½ pint) stock (page 24) or water
1 tablespoon cornflour mixed with a little water
fresh coriander, to garnish (optional)

Scale, gut and clean the fish, if necessary. Dry thoroughly, then score both sides as deep as the bone with criss-cross diagonal cuts, at 1 cm (½ inch) intervals.

Heat the oil in a very hot wok or large frying pan until smoking. Fry the fish on both sides for 3-4 minutes or until golden brown. Push the fish to one side of the wok or pan and add ginger, spring onions, salt, sugar, soy sauce, wine and stock or water. Stir and bring to the boil, then return the fish to the centre, reducing the heat a little. Gently braise for 4-5 minutes, turning the fish over once or twice and basting occasionally.

When the sauce is reduced by half, remove the fish very carefully to a serving platter. Add the cornflour and water mixture to thicken the sauce, stirring until smooth, then pour it over the fish. Garnish with fresh coriander leaves or more spring onions. Serve immediately.

Seafood Casserole

Another speciality from the Cantonese cuisine, this dish is a cross between bouillabaisse and paella, in which several different kinds of fish and/or shellfish are cooked together with vegetables. Exactly what goes into the casserole varies according to the district and seasonal availability.

500 g (1 lb) assorted fish steaks or cutlets, such as cod, haddock, monkfish, whiting, salmon or eel; do not use more than 3 different fish
1 teaspoon salt
1 egg white, lightly beaten
2 tablespoons cornflour mixed with a little water
225 g (8 oz) assorted shellfish, such as prawns, scallops, mussels, oysters or whelks; do not use more than 2 shellfish
3-4 dried Chinese mushrooms, soaked
50 g (2 oz) lean pork
600 ml (1 pint) oil for deep-frying
2-3 cakes bean curd (tofu)
2-3 slices peeled fresh root ginger
2 spring onions, thinly shredded
2 tablespoons light soy sauce
1 teaspoon sugar
2 tablespoons Shao Hsing rice wine or dry sherry
225 ml (8 fl oz) stock (page 24) or water
4-6 Chinese cabbage or lettuce leaves
salt and ground Sichuan pepper
fresh coriander, to garnish

Coat the fish with the salt, egg and cornflour. Shell or peel the shellfish as necessary, then clean and pat dry.

Squeeze dry the mushrooms, discarding the stalks, then thinly shred them. Thinly shred the pork.

Heat the oil in a wok or deep-fat fryer until smoking. Cut each cake of bean curd into 6-8 pieces and deep-fry them for 3-4 minutes or until golden all over, turning gently with a pair of chopsticks or tongs; remove and drain well on kitchen paper. Deep-fry the fish steaks in the same oil for 2-3 minutes or until golden; remove and drain.

Pour off the excess oil, leaving about 1 tablespoon in the wok. Flavour the oil with the ginger and spring onions, then stir-fry the shredded pork and mushrooms for about 30 seconds. Return the bean curd and fish to the wok, then add soy sauce, sugar, wine and stock. Bring to the boil, stirring very gently. Transfer all the ingredients to a Chinese sand-pot or casserole lined with cabbage or lettuce leaves, placing the shellfish on top. Bring to the boil once more over high heat, then reduce the heat and simmer, covered, for 15-20 minutes; do not over-cook.

To serve, remove the sand-pot or casserole from heat, adjust the seasonings and garnish with coriander leaves.

Note: This is most delicious, as well as being light in texture, low in calories and very high in protein.

Cantonese Lobster in Black Bean Sauce

Try to use live lobsters if you can. The flesh of precooked lobsters has been boiled too long, loosing much of its delicate flavour and texture.

1 large or 2 medium lobsters, about 1 kg (2¼ lb) in total
2 tablespoons Shao Hsing rice wine or dry sherry
1 tablespoon light or dark soy sauce
1 tablespoon cornflour
3-4 tablespoons oil
1 clove garlic, finely chopped
1 teaspoon finely chopped peeled fresh root ginger
2-3 spring onions, finely chopped
2 tablespoons salted black beans, coarsely crushed with 1 tablespoon rice wine
1 tablespoon vinegar
75 ml (3 fl oz) stock (page 24) or water

Provided you possess a very sharp knife (a Chinese cleaver is ideal) and the necessary nerves, the best way of killing a live lobster is to cut its head in half lengthways, then work your way down the body until you reach the tail, so you end up with two halves from head to tail. Next, carefully remove the two claws and crack them with the back of a cleaver. The only parts to be discarded are the feathery lungs and intestine. The dark green juices in the head should be kept; they turn bright orange when cooked and are most delicious. Cut each half into 4-5 pieces.

Marinate the lobster pieces in the wine, soy sauce and cornflour for 10-15 minutes.

Heat the oil in a preheated wok or frying pan until smoking. Add the garlic, ginger and spring onions to flavour the oil, then add the black beans, mashing them in the wok with the back of a wooden spoon or spatula until smooth. Add the lobster pieces, stirring constantly for about 2 minutes, then add the vinegar and stock or water. Continue stirring until well blended. When the colour of the lobster is bright orange and the sauce has thickened, serve immediately.

Seafood Casserole (top); Red-Cooked Fish (bottom).

Quick Stir-Fried Dishes

The unique Chinese cooking method known as quick stir-frying has become very popular in western kitchens in recent years. Doubtless, this is because most stir-fried dishes are comparatively simple and easy to prepare and cook, as well as being economical, delicious and healthy.

Basically, all the ingredients are thinly sliced or shredded, then tossed and stirred in a little hot oil over high heat for a very short time. This way meats, such as pork, lamb and beef, can be cooked in 1½-2 minutes; chicken and fish often in less than half that time. High heat and short cooking time also helps to preserve the natural flavours and retain the subtle textures of the food. When correctly done, the meats should be tender and juicy, and the vegetables crisp and bright – overcooking will only make the food a soggy mess.

As can be expected, quick stir-fried dishes form the backbone of everyday Chinese cooking. An inexpensive but delicious and healthy meal of 2-3 stir-fried dishes for 4-6 people (when served with rice or noodles) can be prepared, cooked and served in under one hour, provided you have selected the right materials, and planned your procedure with careful consideration in advance!

There are a number of variations in stir-frying, generally they are classified as follows:

1. Pure stir-frying: The ingredients are not precooked or marinated; they are just stir-fried in hot oil and seasoned towards the end of cooking. Most vegetables are cooked using this method.

2. Rapid stir-frying: This method is known in Chinese as *bao*, which literally means 'to explode'. It requires extreme high heat; the ingredients have been deep-fried or rapid-boiled first, then quickly stir-fried over intense heat for a very short time. The vital point here is to have the seasonings prepared in advance so each step can be performed in quick succession. Variations within this method include **Rapid stir-frying in oil, Rapid stir-frying in bean paste** and **Rapid stir-frying with spring onions.**

3. Braising stir-frying: The main and supplementary ingredients are cooked separately first, then brought together with the addition of seasonings, stock or a thickening agent, such as cornflour mixed with water, and braised very quickly before serving.

4. 'Twice-cooked' stir-frying: One ingredient has previously been cooked and is then cut into smaller pieces and stir-fried with other ingredients and seasonings.

The secret of successful stir-frying lies in the degree of heat and timing. Some people believe if they have all the necessary ingredients and seasonings, and if they follow a good recipe, they cannot fail. In reality, however, the degree of heat is so crucial that sometimes even the difference of a few seconds cooking time can drastically affect the final result.

No precise cooking time can be given for a particular dish because so much depends on the type of cooker, wok or pan you use, and the size you cut your ingredients. After a little practise you will be able to judge the correct timing quite easily.

These subtle and fine points cannot be written in a recipe,

so I advise you to use your eyes, nose and ears to judge while you are cooking. Once you have mastered the subtleties of heat control, the new world of successful Chinese stir-frying is wide open to you.

Sliced Chicken and Vegetables

This recipe originated from Shanghai but is very popular throughout China. It is very quick to make and can be served as the main part of a Chinese meal or on its own for a family supper. The chicken can be, and often is, substituted by other tender meat, such as pork, beef, liver or kidney.

225-275 g (8-10 oz) chicken breast, boned and skinned
1 tablespoon Shao Hsing rice wine or dry sherry
1½ teaspoons salt
½ egg white, lightly beaten
1 tablespoon cornflour mixed with 1 tablespoon water
4-5 dried Chinese mushrooms, soaked (page 10)
100 g (4 oz) bamboo shoots
100 g (4 oz) green vegetable, such as Chinese cabbage or mange-tout
4 tablespoons oil
2 spring onions, cut into short lengths
1 slice fresh root ginger, peeled and cut into 3-4 small pieces
1 teaspoon sugar
1 tablespoon light soy sauce
a little stock or water (optional)
1 teaspoon sesame seed oil

Cut the chicken breasts into thin slices about the size of a postage stamp.

Mix the wine with a pinch of salt, egg white and about half of the cornflour and water mixture. Add the prepared chicken pieces.

Squeeze the mushrooms dry and discard the hard stalks, then cut into pieces about the same size as the chicken. Also cut the bamboo shoots and green vegetable into small pieces about the size of the chicken slices.

Heat the oil in a very hot wok or frying pan until smoking, then reduce the heat and let the oil cool down a little before stir-frying the chicken slices for about 30 seconds or until the colour changes from pink to white. If using pork for this dish, it will require about twice as long cooking time. Also, the heat should not be reduced but kept high all the time; beef, liver or kidney need only same cooking time as chicken, but over high heat. Remove with a slotted spoon and set aside.

Increase the heat to high again, then add the spring onions, ginger and the vegetables, stirring for about 30 seconds. Add the salt, sugar and the chicken together with soy sauce and continue stirring for another minute, adding a little stock or water only if necessary. Finally, add the remaining cornflour and water mixture and stir to thicken the gravy.

Serve hot, garnished with sesame seed oil.

Sliced Chicken and Vegetables.

Shredded Chicken with Celery

One of my personal favourites, this simple dish contrasts the delicate tender chicken with the crunchy and crisp texture of the celery.

2 chicken breasts, boned and skinned
1 teaspoon salt
½ egg white, lightly beaten
2 teaspoons cornflour mixed with a little water
1 celery heart, or 3-4 tender celery stalks
1-2 red or green hot chillies, seeded
600 ml (1 pint) oil for deep-frying
2 spring onions, thinly shredded
2 slices fresh root ginger, peeled and thinly shredded
1 teaspoon sugar
1 tablespoon light soy sauce
1 tablespoon Shao Hsing rice wine or dry sherry

Remove the white tendon and membrane from the chicken breasts, then very thinly shred the breasts into slivers the size of matchsticks. Mix first with a pinch of salt, then the egg white, and finally the cornflour and water mixture, blending well with your fingers.

Thinly shred the celery the same size as the chicken. Cut the chillies into fine shreds.

Heat the oil in a preheated wok or deep-fat fryer until moderately hot. Reduce the heat and add the chicken shreds, stirring gently with chopsticks to separate. As soon as the colour changes from pink to white, remove with a slotted spoon or strainer and set aside to drain on kitchen paper.

Pour off the excess oil, leaving about 2 tablespoons in the wok. Increase the heat to high again and add the chillies, spring onions, ginger and celery, stirring for about 30 seconds. Return the chicken to the wok with the salt, sugar, soy sauce and wine, stirring constantly for about 1 minute more. Blend well and serve hot.

Diced Chicken with Green Peppers

I learnt this dish from my mother, who in turn learnt it from her mother from Jiangxi in south-eastern China.

2 chicken breasts, boned and skinned
1½ teaspoons salt
½ egg white, lightly beaten
2 teaspoons cornflour mixed with 1 tablespoon water
1-2 green peppers, cored and seeded
4 tablespoons oil
2 spring onions, cut into short lengths
1 teaspoon sugar
1 tablespoon Shao Hsing rice wine or dry sherry
a little stock or water (optional)
a few drops sesame seed oil

Remove the white tendon and membrane from the chicken breasts, then cut into small cubes the size of sugar lumps. Mix with a pinch of the salt, then the egg white and finally the cornflour and water mixture, blending well with your fingers.

Cut the green peppers to the same size as the chicken cubes. (For extra colour, you can use a red pepper in addition to a green one.)

Heat the oil in a very hot wok or frying pan until smoking. Reduce the heat and let the oil cool down a little before stir-frying the chicken cubes for about 30 seconds or until the colour changes from pink to white. Remove with a slotted spoon and carefully drain on kitchen paper.

Increase the heat to high again, add the spring onions followed by the green peppers, stirring for about 30 seconds, then return the chicken cubes to the wok with the salt, sugar and wine; continue stirring for about another minute at most, adding a little stock or water *only* if it's necessary. Add the sesame seed oil as garnish and serve hot.

Stir-Fried Chicken Cubes with Cucumber

The cucumber is peeled in this orthodox recipe from Canton, but very often I leave the skin on to give the dish an extra colour, as well as a stronger flavour.

2 chicken breasts, boned and skinned
1 teaspoon salt
½ egg white, lightly beaten
2 teaspoons cornflour mixed with a little cold water
1 medium cucumber, about 30 cm (12 inches) long
4 tablespoons oil
1-2 cloves garlic, crushed
2 spring onions, cut into short lengths
1 tablespoon Shao Hsing rice wine or dry sherry
1 tablespoon light soy sauce
a few drops sesame seed oil

Remove the white tendon and membrane from the chicken breasts, then dice the meat into small cubes. Mix first with a pinch of the salt, then the egg white, and finally the cornflour and water mixture, blending well with your fingers.

Cut the cucumber roughly the same shape and size as the chicken cubes.

Heat the oil in a very hot wok or frying pan until smoking, then reduce heat and let the oil cool down a little before stir-frying the chicken cubes for 30-40 seconds or until the colour changes from pink to white. Remove with a slotted spoon.

Turn the heat back to high, add the garlic, spring onions, cucumber and salt and stir-fry for about 30 seconds. Return the chicken cubes to the pan with the wine and soy sauce, and continue stirring for another minute at the most. Add the sesame seed oil, blending well. Serve hot.

Shredded Chicken with Celery (left); Diced Chicken with Green Peppers (right).

Chicken Fu-Yung

As I have explained previously, *fu-yung* in Chinese means creamy-textured egg whites. It is often lightly deep-fried, which prompted certain imaginative cooks to call this dish 'deep-fried milk'!

100 g (4 oz) chicken breast with bone
1 tablespoon cornflour mixed with 1 tablespoon cold water
5-6 egg whites, lightly beaten
25 ml (1 fl oz) milk
1 teaspoon salt
600 ml (1 pint) oil for deep-frying
125 ml (4 fl oz) chicken stock
1 tablespoon Shao Hsing rice wine or dry sherry
25 g (1 oz) green peas
25 g (1 oz) cooked ham, finely chopped
a few drops of sesame seed oil

Ideally, use the two tenderest strips of chicken meat just along the breastbone. Remove the bone and pound the meat by using the blunt edge of the cleaver for about 5 minutes, adding a little cold water occasionally. Chop the meat for a further 5-10 minutes or until the meat has a creamy texture.

Make a smooth batter with the cornflour and water mixture, chicken meat, egg whites, milk and a pinch of salt, blending well.

Heat the oil in a very hot wok or deep-fat fryer until smoking, then turn off the heat to cool down the oil to moderately hot before pouring in the mixture, spoonful by spoonful. When all has been added, turn the heat to moderate and stir the oil up from the bottom of the pan to help the fu-yung rise, making sure not to touch them or they will scatter. As soon as they are set, scoop out with a slotted spoon or strainer and drain well on kitchen paper. Place on a serving dish.

Pour off the excess oil, turn up the heat to high again and bring the stock to the boil, then add the salt, wine and green peas and thicken with a little more cornflour and water mixture. Pour it over the fu-yung. Sprinkle over the finely-chopped ham and sesame seed oil as a garnish. Serve hot with a spoon.

Sichuan 'Kung-Po' Chicken with Cashews

Sichuan 'Kung-Po' Chicken with Cashews (left); Sichuan Shredded Beef with Celery and Carrots (right).

This is a very popular dish named after a court official from Sichuan. The cashews can be substituted with walnuts, peanuts or almonds.

275-350 g (10-12 oz) chicken meat, boned and skinned
½ teaspoon salt
1 egg white, lightly beaten
1 tablespoon cornflour mixed with 1 tablespoon water
1 green pepper, cored and seeded
50 g (2 oz) shelled cashew nuts
4 tablespoons oil
2 spring onions, cut into short lengths
1-2 slices fresh root ginger, peeled and cut into several small pieces
3-4 dried red chillies, soaked in warm water for 10 minutes
1 tablespoon sweet bean paste (Hoi Sin sauce) or
*   1 tablespoon Sichuan chilli bean paste mixed with*
*   1 teaspoon sugar*
2 tablespoons Shao Hsing rice wine or dry sherry

Cut the chicken meat into small cubes about the size of sugar lumps. Mix first with the salt, then the egg white and finally about half of the cornflour and water mixture, blending well with your fingers.

Cut the green peppers into the same size as the chicken cubes. Split the cashew nuts into halves.

Heat the oil in a preheated wok or frying pan until smoking. Stir-fry the chicken cubes for about 30 seconds or until the colour changes from pink to white, then remove with a slotted spoon.

To the same hot oil, add the spring onions, ginger, chillies and cashew nuts, followed by the bean sauce, stirring a few times. Add the green peppers and chicken cubes and continue stirring for about 30 seconds, then add the wine and stir-fry for about 30 seconds more. Finally, thicken the gravy with the remaining cornflour and water mixture, blending well. Serve hot.

Sichuan Shredded Beef with Celery and Carrots

This is a highly aromatic and spicy dish. The rather unusual method of cooking is unique to Sichuan.

275 g (10 oz) braising beef steak
2-3 celery stalks
2-3 carrots
3 tablespoons sesame seed oil
2 tablespoons Shao Hsing rice wine or dry sherry
1 tablespoon chilli bean paste
1 tablespoon sweet bean paste
1 clove garlic, crushed and finely chopped
½ teaspoon salt
1 tablespoon sugar
2 spring onions, finely chopped
2 slices fresh root ginger, peeled and finely chopped
ground Sichuan pepper and chilli oil to taste

Thinly shred the beef to the size of matchsticks. Thinly shred the celery and carrots to the same size.

Heat the sesame seed oil in a preheated wok or frying pan, but before the oil gets too hot, reduce the heat and stir-fry the beef shreds until they are separated. Add about 1 tablespoon wine and increase the heat to high, then continue stirring until all the liquid is evaporated and the beef is absolutely dry. Add the chilli bean paste, sweet bean paste, garlic, salt, sugar and more wine, stirring over moderate heat for about 30 seconds. Increase the heat to high again and add the celery, carrots, spring onions and ginger, stirring for another minute. Add the pepper and chilli oil, blending well. Serve hot!

Stir-Fried Beef with Onions

In China, onions are known as 'foreign' onions, indicating their origin is quite different to the native spring onions.

225-275 g (8-10 oz) beef steak, such as rump
1 tablespoon light or dark soy sauce
½ teaspoon ground Sichuan pepper
1 tablespoon Shao Hsing rice wine or dry sherry
1 teaspoon cornflour mixed with a little water
3 medium or 2 large onions
600 ml (1 pint) oil for deep-frying
2-3 slices peeled fresh root ginger, thinly shredded
1 teaspoon salt
a few drops sesame seed oil

Cut the beef into thin strips the size of potato chips, then marinate in a glass bowl with the soy sauce, pepper, wine and cornflour for 25-30 minutes. Thinly slice the onions.

Heat the oil in a wok or deep-fat fryer until smoking, then reduce the heat and let the oil cool down a little before stirring in the beef, separating the strips with chopsticks or a carving fork. Fry for about 30 seconds or until the colour of the meat changes, then remove with a slotted spoon or strainer and drain well on kitchen paper.

Pour off the excess oil, leaving about 2 tablespoons in the wok. Increase the heat to high again, and when the oil is hot, stir-fry the ginger with the onions and salt until the onions become translucent. Return the beef and continue stirring for about 1 minute. Garnish with sesame seed oil and serve hot.

Sliced Beef in Oyster Sauce

Oyster sauce is a Cantonese speciality, and the main feature of this dish is its extreme tenderness and savoury flavour. Any cut of steak can be used, but a long marinating time is more important with cheaper cuts.

275-350 g (10-12 oz) beef steak, such as rump
1 teaspoon sugar
1 tablespoon soy sauce
1 tablespoon Shao Hsing rice wine or dry sherry
2 teaspoons cornflour mixed with a little water
1 small Chinese cabbage or cos lettuce
4-5 tablespoons oil
2 spring onions, cut into short lengths
1 slice peeled fresh root ginger, cut into 3-4 small pieces
½ teaspoon salt
2 tablespoons oyster sauce

Thinly slice the beef, then cut into pieces about the size of a large postage stamp.

Mix with the sugar, soy sauce, wine and cornflour and marinate in a glass bowl for at least 1-2 hours; the longer the marinating, the more tender the beef will be.

Wash the cabbage or lettuce and cut each leaf into 2-3 slices.

Heat the oil in a very hot wok or frying pan until smoking. Stir-fry the beef for about 30 seconds or until the colour changes. Quickly remove with a slotted spoon and set aside. Add the spring onions and ginger and stir-fry with the cabbage or lettuce and salt. As soon as the leaves are limp, return the beef together with the oyster sauce, stirring for about 30 seconds to blend well. Overcooking will toughen the beef.

Serve immediately.

Beef and Green Peppers in Black Bean Sauce

This is another Cantonese dish, though both the Peking and Sichuan restaurants have it on their menus.

225-275 g (8-10 oz) beef steak, such as rump
1 tablespoon soy sauce
1 tablespoon Shao Hsing rice wine or dry sherry
1 teaspoon sugar
1 teaspoon cornflour mixed with a little water
1 large or 2 small green peppers, cored and seeded
1 large or 2 small onions
4 tablespoons oil
2 spring onions, cut into short lengths
1 slice peeled fresh root ginger, cut into small pieces
1-2 green or red hot chillies, seeded and thinly sliced
2 tablespoons crushed black beans

Cut the beef into thin slices about the size of a large postage stamp, then marinate with the soy sauce, wine, sugar and cornflour for 25-30 minutes. Slice the green peppers and onions into the same size as the beef.

Heat the oil in a preheated wok or frying pan until smoking. Stir-fry the beef for about 30 seconds, then quickly remove with a slotted spoon and set aside. In the same oil, add the spring onions, ginger, chillies, green pepper and onions. Stir for a few times, then add the black beans and beef, blending well. Stir constantly for 1 minute at the most. Serve hot.

Stir-Fried Kidney 'Flowers' with Vegetables

This recipe originated in Shandong, and is one of my favourites. Some people dislike the strong flavour of kidneys, but if you remove the fat and white, tough parts in the middle before cooking, you will find kidneys have a most delicate taste.

225-275 g (8-10 oz) pig's kidneys
1 teaspoon salt
2 teaspoons cornflour mixed with 1 tablespoon cold water
15 g (½ oz) wood ears
50 g (2 oz) water chestnuts
100 g (4 oz) bamboo shoots
100 g (4 oz) seasonal green vegetable, such as cabbage, lettuce or spinach
about 600 ml (1 pint) oil for deep-frying
1 clove garlic, crushed
1 spring onion, finely chopped
1 teaspoon finely chopped peeled fresh ginger root ginger
2 teaspoons vinegar
1 tablespoon soy sauce, light or dark
1 tablespoon Shao Hsing rice wine or dry sherry

Split kidneys in half lengthways and discard the white and tough parts in the middle. Score the surface of the kidneys about two-thirds the way down in a fine criss-cross pattern, then cut them into oblong postage stamp-sized pieces; when cooked they will open up and resemble ears of corn – hence the name of 'flowers' for this dish. Marinate for at least 15-20 minutes with a pinch of salt and about half of the cornflour and water mixture.

Soak the wood ears in warm water for about 15-20 minutes. Cut the water chestnuts and bamboo shoots into small, thin slices. Rinse the wood ears and discard the hard bits. Blanch the green vegetables.

Heat the oil in a wok or deep-fat fryer until very hot. Deep-fry the kidney pieces for 10-15 seconds only, stirring with a pair of cooking chopsticks or a carving fork to separate the pieces. Quickly remove with a slotted spoon or strainer and drain well on kitchen paper.

Pour off the excess oil, leaving about 2 tablespoons in the wok. Throw in the garlic, spring onions and ginger, then add the vinegar, vegetables and kidney, stirring for about 1 minute. Add the salt, soy sauce and wine. Finally, add the remaining cornflour and water mixture, blending well until thick. Serve hot.

Sichuan 'Kung-Po' Kidneys

This is a hot and sour version of the kidney 'flowers' from Sichuan.

400 g (14 oz) pig's kidneys
½ teaspoon salt
¼ teaspoon ground Sichuan pepper
1 tablespoon Shao Hsing rice wine or dry sherry
1 teaspoon cornflour mixed with 2 teaspoons water
5-6 dried red chillies, soaked in warm water for 10 minutes
2-3 spring onions
1 clove garlic, crushed
2 slices peeled fresh root ginger
about 600 ml (1 pint) oil for deep-frying
a few drops sesame seed oil

Sauce:
1 tablespoon soy sauce
1 tablespoon vinegar
1 tablespoon sugar
3-4 tablespoons stock (page 24) or water
2 teaspoons cornflour

Split the kidneys in half lengthways and discard the white and tough parts in the middle. Score the surface of the kidneys about two-thirds the way down in a fine criss-cross pattern, then cut them into oblong postage stamp-sized pieces. Marinate the pieces with salt, pepper, wine and cornflour while you prepare the vegetables.

Cut the chillies into small pieces, discarding the seeds; cut the spring onions into short lengths and finely chop the garlic and ginger. Mix together the sauce ingredients in a bowl or jug.

Heat the oil in a wok or deep-fat fryer until hot. Deep-fry the kidney pieces for about 1 minute, stirring to separate them, then quickly remove and drain well on kitchen paper.

Pour off the excess oil, leaving about 1 tablespoon in the wok. Add the chillies and fry until brown, then add the garlic, spring onions, ginger and the kidneys. Stir a few times, then add the sauce mixture, blending well. As soon as the sauce starts to bubble, add the sesame seed oil.

Serve immediately.

Stir-Fried Liver Slices and Wood Ears

The contrast between the crunchiness of the fungus and the tender softness of the liver makes this dish extremely popular. Because of the delicate texture, liver should never be overcooked.

25 g (1 oz) wood ears
275-350 g (10-12 oz) pig's liver
2-3 spring onions
3-4 tablespoons oil
1 tablespoon light or dark soy sauce
1 teaspoon cornflour mixed with a little water
salt and pepper

Soak the wood ears in warm water for about 15-20 minutes. Rinse in cold water, then tear the large ones into smaller pieces, discarding any hard stalks.

Wash the liver and wipe dry on kitchen paper. Discard the white membrane, then cut into match-box sized thin pieces. Cut the spring onions into short lengths.

Mix the soy sauce into the cornflour and water mixture.

Heat the oil in a very hot wok or frying pan until smoking.

While waiting for the oil to smoke, quickly pour some boiling water over the liver in a large bowl, stir to separate each piece, drain through a sieve, then mix the liver with soy sauce and cornflour and water mixture.

Add the liver to the hot oil and stir-fry for about 30 seconds, then add the spring onions and wood ears together with the salt. Stir for 30 seconds at the most. The crucial points here are timing and heat control: remember not to overcook the liver and to keep the heat as high as you possibly can – and keep your cool at the same time!

Serve immediately.

Stir-Fried Kidney 'Flowers' with Vegetables (top); Stir-Fried Liver Slices and Wood Ears (bottom).

Eggs with Tomatoes

This is a very colourful and delicious dish, and very simple to make. Ideally you should use hard, green tomatoes, but they are not so easy to come by unless you grow your own; try to get the most under-ripe and firm ones if possible. Other vegetables, such as cucumbers, green peppers or peas, can be substituted for the tomatoes.

275 g (10 oz) under-ripe tomatoes
4-5 eggs
1½ teaspoons salt
2 spring onions, finely chopped
4 tablespoons oil

Slice the tomatoes. Beat the eggs with a pinch of salt and about one-third of the finely chopped spring onions.

Heat half the oil in a very hot wok or frying pan. Reduce the heat and lightly scramble the eggs until set but not too hard; remove and set aside. Increase the heat to high again and heat the remaining oil until smoking, then add the remaining finely chopped spring onions and tomatoes. Stir for about 30 seconds with salt, then return the scrambled eggs to the wok and continue stirring for about 30 seconds. This dish is best served hot.

Quick-Braised Chinese Cabbage with Mushrooms

Also known as Chinese leaves or *bok choy*, Chinese cabbage has pale-green, curly leaves with a long white stem. A different species has a shorter and fatter head with pale-yellow leaves. Both will keep fresh for a long time and retain the crunchy texture even after lengthy cooking.

400 g (14 oz) Chinese cabbage
350 g (12 oz) canned straw mushrooms, or 225 g (8 oz) fresh button
  mushrooms
3-4 tablespoons oil
1½ teaspoons salt
1 teaspoon sugar
125 ml (4 fl oz) stock (page 24)
1 tablespoon cornflour mixed with 3 tablespoons milk

Separate the cabbage leaves and cut each leaf in half lengthways. Drain the canned straw mushrooms; if using fresh ones, do not peel, just trim off the stalks.

Heat the oil in a preheated wok or frying pan. Stir-fry the cabbage for about 1 minute, then add 1 teaspoon salt and sugar. Continue stirring for about 1 minute, then add the stock (or water if stock is not available). Bring to the boil, then remove the cabbage with a slotted spoon and arrange neatly on one side of a serving dish.

Add the mushrooms with the remaining salt and braise for about 1 minute. Thicken the sauce with the cornflour and milk mixture, stirring until smooth. Remove the mushrooms with a slotted spoon and place them next to the cabbage on the plate. Pour the creamy sauce evenly all over the cabbage and mushrooms. Serve hot.

Note: 425 g (15 oz) fresh or canned asparagus spears can be used instead of, or as well as, Chinese cabbage for this dish.

Most vegetables can be stir-fried; choose a selection with contrasting colours and textures.

Mixed Vegetables

The Chinese never mix ingredients indiscriminately, but rather different items are carefully selected with the aim of achieving a harmonious balance of colour, aroma, flavour and texture.
The following is a suggested list. Obviously, you do not have to use all of them in the same dish, but select 4-6 different items for their contrast in colour and texture.

25 g (1 oz) wood ears
225 g (8 oz) Chinese cabbage, lettuce or green cabbage
100 g (4 oz) broccoli or cauliflower
100 g (4 oz) straw or oyster mushrooms
100 g (4 oz) baby corn (also known as dwarf or young corn)
100 g (4 oz) courgettes
100 g (4 oz) fresh bean sprouts or celery hearts
1 small green or red pepper, cored and seeded
4 tablespoons oil
1 teaspoon salt
1 teaspoon sugar
a little stock or water (optional)
1 tablespoon light soy sauce
a few drops sesame seed oil (optional)

Soak the wood ears in water for 20-25 minutes, then rinse and discard the hard bits.

Meanwhile, prepare the other vegetables by cutting them into roughly a uniform size, except the bean sprouts, which need only be washed and rinsed (see Stir-Fried Bean Sprouts, below). The mushrooms can also be left whole unless they are exceptionally large, in which case halve or quarter them. If fresh baby corn is not available, canned corn can be used; leave whole if tiny, otherwise cut each one into 3-4 small diamond-shaped pieces.

Heat the oil in a preheated wok or large frying pan until smoking. Add the cabbage, broccoli or cauliflower, baby corns and courgettes, stirring for about 30 seconds before adding the remaining vegetables. Continue stirring for about 30 seconds, then add the salt, sugar and a little stock or water, if necessary. Toss and turn until well blended, then add the soy sauce and cook for 1 minute at the very most. Add the sesame seed oil, if using.

Serve hot or cold.

Stir-Fried Bean Sprouts

Only fresh bean sprouts should be used in all recipes in this book; canned bean sprouts will not have the crispness or the flavour of the fresh ones.

500 g (1 lb) fresh bean sprouts
1-2 spring onions, thinly shredded
3-4 tablespoons oil
1 teaspoon salt
1 teaspoon sugar

Wash and rinse the bean sprouts in a bowl of cold water, discard any husks and other bits that float to the surface. Do not top and tail each sprout – that would take you hours.

Heat the oil in a preheated wok until smoking. Add the spring onions and stir a few times, then add the bean sprouts and stir-fry for about 30 seconds. Add the salt and sugar and continue stirring for about another 30 seconds. Do not overcook, otherwise the sprouts will become soggy.

This dish can be served either hot or cold.

Stir-Fried French Beans

French beans, runner beans or mange-tout can be cooked exactly the same way, provided they are young and tender. Avoid buying wilted or overly mature beans with tough-looking pods; they are usually too stringy and tasteless.

500 g (1 lb) green beans
3 tablespoons oil
1 teaspoon salt
1 teaspoon sugar
a little stock or water (optional)
2 teaspoons light soy sauce

Thoroughly wash the beans in cold water, then drain. If the beans are fresh and young they will only need to be topped and tailed, but a few may require stringing: slender dwarf beans and small mange-tout can be left whole; larger French beans and mange-tout should be snapped in half; and runner beans may need to be sliced with a knife.

Heat the oil in a very hot wok or large frying pan until smoking. Stir-fry the beans for about 1 minute, then add the salt and sugar, stirring for about another 30 seconds.

Add a little stock or water *only* if necessary. Finally, add the soy sauce and cook for 30 seconds more.

Serve hot or cold.

Note: Extra seasonings, such as crushed garlic, fresh root ginger or hot chillies can be used to flavour the oil before stir-frying the beans, if desired.

Quick-fry of 'Four Precious Vegetables'

The 'Four Precious Vegetables' are chosen for their harmonious contrast in colour and texture.

5-6 dried Chinese mushrooms, soaked
225 g (8 oz) canned bamboo shoots, drained
100 g (4 oz) mange-tout
225 g (8 oz) young carrots
3-4 tablespoons oil
1 teaspoon salt
1 teaspoon sugar
a little stock or water (optional)
1 tablespoon light soy sauce
a few drops sesame seed oil

Squeeze the mushrooms dry and discard the tough stalks, then cut the bamboo shoots into thin slices. Wash, top and tail the mange-tout, leaving them whole if small, otherwise snap in half. Thinly slice the carrots diagonally.

Heat the oil in a preheated wok or large frying pan. Stir-fry the carrots and mange-tout for about 30 seconds, then add the bamboo shoots and mushrooms. Cook for another minute, then add the salt and sugar, stirring. Add a little stock or water if the vegetables dry out at this stage. Otherwise, just add the soy sauce and sesame seed oil and blend well.

Serve hot or cold.

Stir-Fried Green Cabbage

The cabbage season lasts almost all year round: from April to the end of summer you have the oval-shaped spring greens; from September to February you have winter cabbage, which is round with a firm heart. Yet in between these two seasons there are enough varieties, some early and some late, to ensure a good sequence.

750 g (1½ lb) green cabbage
3-4 tablespoons vegetable oil
2-3 small pieces peeled fresh root ginger (optional)
1 teaspoon salt
1 teaspoon sugar
1 tablespoon light soy sauce
a little stock or water (optional)

Choose a cabbage that is young and fresh, discarding any outer, tough leaves. Wash it in cold water *before* cutting into thin strips like sauerkraut or coleslaw.

Preheat a wok or large frying pan. Add the oil and swirl it in the wok to cover most of the area, and when the oil starts to smoke, throw in the ginger pieces (if using) to flavour the oil for a few seconds. Add the cabbage, stirring constantly for about 1 minute. Add the salt and sugar and continue stirring for about 30 seconds. Add soy sauce and a little stock or water *only* if necessary, then stir a few more times. Do not overcook, otherwise the cabbage will lose its crispness, as well as a great deal of its vitamin content. Be sure to use as high a heat as you possibly can all the time.

Serve immediately.

Quick-fry of 'Four Precious Vegetables'.

Bean curd (*tofu*) with Spinach

This is a very colourful as well as nutritious dish. Try to get small fresh spinach bundles from an Oriental food store; they have much more flavour than the large, pale-green leaves. If using the smaller type, the bright-red root adds extra colour to the dish.

275 g (10 oz) fresh spinach
3 cakes bean curd (tofu)
4 tablespoons oil
1 clove garlic, crushed
1 teaspoon salt
1 teaspoon sugar
1 tablespoon soy sauce
a few drops of sesame seed oil

Thoroughly wash the spinach and shake off as much excess water as possible.

Cut each bean curd cake into about 8-10 pieces.

Heat the oil in a very hot wok or frying pan until smoking. Fry the bean curd pieces for about 3-4 minutes, very gently, turning over once or twice, then remove with a slotted spoon and set aside.

Flavour the oil with the crushed garlic and stir-fry the spinach for about 30 seconds or until the leaves are limp. Add the bean curd pieces, salt, sugar and soy sauce. Blend well by stirring very gently and cook for another 1-1½ minutes.

Add the sesame seed oil and serve immediately.

Stir-Fried Lettuce Hearts

The upright cos lettuce with a firm heart is best for this recipe; if you use round or cabbage lettuce, choose a Webb's wonder or iceberg with crisp leaves; the floppy, soft butterheads can also be used, but then you will probably need more than two or three.

1 large or 2-3 small heads lettuce
3 tablespoons oil
½ teaspoon salt
1 teaspoon sugar
1 tablespoon oyster sauce, or 2 teaspoons light soy sauce

Separate the lettuce leaves, discarding the tough outer leaves. Wash the heart in cold water, if necessary. Cut in quarters lengthways, or in 6-8 segments if using a large, round head, then shake off the excess water as you would when making a salad.

Preheat a wok or large frying pan over high fire until very hot. Add the oil and wait until it starts to smoke. Swirl the wok so about three-quarters of the surface is well greased. Add the lettuce heart (this will make a loud noise, do not be alarmed) and stir vigorously until all the leaves are coated with oil, just as you would when mixing and tossing salad with dressing.

Add salt and sugar, stir a few times more until the noise becomes less and the leaves become slightly limp.

Add the oyster sauce or soy sauce, then quickly serve. Make sure you do not overcook, otherwise the lettuce will lose its crispness and bright green colour.

This dish can be served cold.

Braised Aubergine

Choose the slender, purple variety of aubergine, rather than the large round kind, if possible. This recipe comes from Shanghai in eastern China.

500 g (1 lb) aubergine
600 ml (1 pint) oil for deep-frying
2 cloves garlic, crushed
1 teaspoon finely chopped peeled fresh root ginger
1 tablespoon light or dark soy sauce
2 tablespoons sweet bean paste (Hoi Sin Sauce), or
    1 tablespoon crushed yellow bean sauce, mixed with
      2 teaspoons sugar
a little stock or water (optional)
1 teaspoon cornflour mixed with 1 tablespoon water
1 teaspoon sesame seed oil

Remove the stems from the aubergines, then, without peeling, diagonally cut into slices about 2.5 cm (1 inch) thick.

Heat the oil in a wok or deep-fat fryer until hot. Deep-fry the aubergines for 1-1½ minutes, remove with slotted spoon and drain on kitchen paper.

Pour off the excess oil, leaving about 1 tablespoon in the wok. Add the garlic and ginger, stirring a few times, then return the aubergines with the soy sauce and bean paste. Braise over moderate heat for about 2 minutes, adding a little stock or water, if necessary, stirring occasionally. Thicken the gravy with the cornflour and water mixture and add the sesame seed oil, blending well. Serve hot or cold.

Twice-Cooked Pork, Sichuan Style

This is another Sichuan dish that has become popular not only in the rest of China, but throughout the world. Any leftovers from Crystal-Boiled Pork (page 21) can be used instead of cooking fresh meat.

500 g (1 lb) leg of pork, boned but not skinned
1 small green pepper, cored and seeded
100 g (4 oz) bamboo shoots
3 tablespoons oil
2 spring onions, cut into short lengths
1 teaspoon salt
1 teaspoon sugar
1 tablespoon soy sauce
1 tablespoon chilli bean sauce
1 tablespoon Shao Hsing rice wine or dry sherry

Place the whole piece of pork in a saucepan and cover with water. Bring it to the boil, then simmer for about 40 minutes. Turn off the heat and leave the meat in the liquid, with the skin side up, for at least 2-3 hours, covered, before removing it to cool.

Just before cooking, skin the pork, and, if you are calorie-conscious, trim off some of the excess fat. Thinly slice and cut into pieces about the size of a large postage stamp. Cut the green pepper and bamboo shoots into small slices.

Heat the oil in a preheated wok or frying pan until smoking. Add the spring onions, green peppers and bamboo shoots, stirring for a few seconds. Add the salt, sugar and pork and continue stirring for a few more seconds, then add the soy sauce, chilli bean sauce and wine. Blend well and stir-fry for another minute. Serve hot.

Stir-Fried Pork with Mange-Tout

This is a basic recipe for stir-frying pork with any fresh, young vegetables. For instance, mange-tout can be replaced by broccoli, green peppers, cabbage, asparagus, green beans or courgettes.

225 g (8 oz) lean pork fillet or steak
1 tablespoon light soy sauce
1 tablespoon Shao Hsing rice wine
2 teaspoons cornflour mixed with 1 tablespoon water
225 g (8 oz) mange-tout or any other young vegetable
4 tablespoons oil
1-2 spring onions, cut into short lengths
1 slice peeled fresh root ginger, cut into small pieces
1 teaspoon salt
1 teaspoon sugar
a little stock or water (optional)

Thinly slice the pork and cut into pieces about the size of an oblong postage stamp. Mix with soy sauce and cornflour mixture and set aside to marinate while preparing the mange-tout.

If the mange-tout are fresh and young, they will not be stringy and therefore will only need to be topped and tailed; leave whole if small, otherwise snap larger ones in half. Cut other vegetables into small slices or pieces about the same size as the pork.

Heat the oil in a preheated wok or frying pan until smoking. Stir-fry the pork for about 1 minute or until the colour of the meat changes, then remove with a slotted spoon and set aside. Add the spring onions to the wok to flavour the oil for a few seconds before adding the mange-tout, stirring vigorously for a few times, then add the salt, sugar and return the pork to the pan. Continue stirring for 1-1½ minutes depending on the type of the cooker and/or the size and thickness of the ingredients; add a little stock or water *only* if necessary. Do not overcook or the meat will be tough and the vegetables will be soggy.

Diced Lamb in Peking Sweet Bean Sauce

It is said that this is the original 'sweet and sour' dish from the Yellow River valley in north China.

275-350 g (10-12 oz) leg of lamb fillet
1 tablespoon Kao Liang spirit, brandy, rum, or whisky
1 tablespoon yellow bean sauce
2 teaspoons cornflour
½ cucumber, about 15 cm (6 inches) long
600 ml (1 pint) oil for deep-frying
1 teaspoon finely chopped fresh root ginger
½ teaspoon sesame seed oil

Sauce:
1 tablespoon soy sauce
1 tablespoon Shao Hsing rice wine or dry sherry
1 tablespoon vinegar
2 tablespoons sugar
*1 tablespoon cornflour mixed with 3 tablespoons stock (page 24) or
  water*

Trim the excess fat from the lamb, then dice the meat into small cubes the size of sugar lumps. Marinate in a glass bowl with the spirit, yellow bean sauce and cornflour while you prepare the vegetables.

Cut the cucumber into small cubes the same size as the lamb; do not peel the cucumber. Mix all the ingredients for the sauce in a bowl or jug.

Heat the oil in a wok or deep-fat fryer until smoking. Fry the lamb cubes for 25-30 seconds, stirring to separate the cubes. As soon as the colour changes, remove and drain well on kitchen paper.

Pour off the excess oil, leaving about 1 tablespoon in the wok. Add the finely chopped ginger and cucumber, stirring for about 30 seconds, then add the sauce mixture. Stir to make it smooth, then add the lamb cubes. Blend well and serve as soon as each meat cube is coated with the sauce.

Stir-Fried Pork with Mange-Tout (left); Sichuan 'Fish-Flavoured' Shredded Pork (right).

Sichuan 'Fish-Flavoured' Shredded Pork

Like 'Fish-Flavoured' Aubergines (page 64), no fish is actually involved in this dish.

25 g (1 oz) wood ears
275-350 g (10-12 oz) pork fillet
1 teaspoon salt
1 tablespoon cornflour mixed with 1 tablespoon water
2-3 celery stalks or young leeks
4 tablespoons oil
1 clove garlic, crushed and finely chopped
1 teaspoon finely chopped fresh root ginger
2 spring onions, finely chopped
1 tablespoon soy sauce
1 tablespoon chilli bean sauce
1 teaspoon sugar
2 teaspoons vinegar

Soak the wood ears for 25 minutes. Thinly shred the pork into matchstick-sized pieces. Mix with a little salt and about half of the cornflour and water mixture. Rinse the wood ears then thinly shred. Shred the celery or leeks, too.

Heat about half the oil in a preheated wok or frying pan. Stir-fry the pork until the colour changes, then remove. Add the remaining oil and when it is smoking, add the garlic, ginger, spring onions, celery or leeks and wood ears. Stir a few times, then return the pork to the pan with the salt, soy sauce, chilli bean paste, sugar and vinegar. Cook for 1-1½ minutes, stirring constantly. Add the remaining cornflour and water mixture, blending well. Serve hot.

Hunan Braised Bean Curd (Tofu), Family Style

Of the eight provinces that border on Sichuan, only Hunan to the south-east is closely affiliated with the cooking of its distinguished neighbour – they both like hot and spicy food.

4 cakes bean curd (tofu)
100 g (4 oz) lean boneless pork
2 spring onions
5-6 fresh or dried red chillies
600 ml (1 pint) oil for deep-frying
½ teaspoon salt
1 tablespoon yellow, black or sweet bean paste
1 tablespoon light or dark soy sauce
a little water
2 teaspoons cornflour mixed with a little water
a few drops sesame seed oil

Split each cake of bean curd crossways into 3 or 4 thin slices, then cut each slice diagonally into two triangles.

Cut the pork into small, thin slices, cut the spring onions into short lengths and cut the chillies into small pieces.

Heat the oil in a wok or deep-fat fryer until hot. Deep-fry the bean curd triangles for 2-3 minutes or until golden on both sides. Remove with a slotted spoon and drain well on kitchen paper.

Pour off the excess oil, leaving about 1 tablespoon in the wok. Add the pork and stir-fry for about 30 seconds, then add the bean curd, salt, spring onions, chillies, bean paste, soy sauce and a little water. Stir very gently and braise for about 2 minutes, then thicken the sauce with the cornflour and water mixture. Add the sesame seed oil. Serve hot.

Sweet and Sour Pork

This is without doubt one of the best-known dishes served in Chinese restaurants and take-aways. Unfortunately, however, it is too often spoiled by cooks who use too much tomato ketchup for the sauce. Here is an authentic recipe from Canton.

275 g (10 oz) pork, not too lean
½ teaspoon salt
1 tablespoon Kao Liang spirit, brandy, rum or whisky
100 g (4 oz) bamboo shoots
1 small green pepper, cored and seeded
600 ml (1 pint) oil for deep-frying
1 egg, lightly beaten
½ tablespoon cornflour
1 tablespoon plain flour
1 clove garlic, crushed and finely chopped
1 spring onion, cut into short lengths
1 small hot chilli, seeded and thinly shredded (optional)

Sauce
2 tablespoons vinegar
2 tablespoons sugar
1 tablespoon soy sauce
1 tablespoon tomato purée
2 teaspoons cornflour mixed with 2 tablespoons water

Cut the meat into small cubes not much bigger than the size of olives, then marinate in a glass bowl with the salt and spirit for about 1 hour.

Cut the bamboo shoots and green pepper into small pieces about the same size as the pork.

Heat the oil in a wok or deep-fat fryer; while waiting for it to get hot, dust the pork pieces with the cornflour, then dip in the beaten egg, and finally coat each piece with the flour. Lower the meat into the oil, piece by piece, and deep-fry for about 3 minutes. Remove with a slotted spoon or strainer and drain well on kitchen paper. Heat the oil to hot again and return the pork. Fry for 1 minute more or until golden. Remove and drain again.

Pour off the excess oil, leaving about 1 tablespoon in the wok, then add garlic, spring onions, green pepper and bamboo shoots, stirring for a few seconds, then add the sweet and sour sauce mixture. Stir until smooth, then add the pork, blending well until each piece is coated with the translucent sauce. Serve immediately.

Hunan Braised Bean Curd, Family Style (left);
Sweet and Sour Pork (right).

Pork with Bean Sprouts

Obviously, the pork can be interchanged with chicken or another kind of meat. I must emphasize once more that you should use only fresh bean sprouts.

225 g (8 oz) fresh bean sprouts
100-175 g (4-6 oz) pork fillet
3-4 tablespoons oil
1 tablespoon light soy sauce
1 tablespoon Shao Hsing rice wine or dry sherry
1-2 spring onions, thinly shredded
1 teaspoon sugar
1 teaspoon salt

Wash and rinse the bean sprouts in a bowl, discarding any husks and bits that float to the surface. Thinly shred the pork into strips as fine as the sprouts.

Heat about 1 tablespoon oil in a very hot wok or frying pan until smoking, then add the pork and stir to separate the shreds. When the colour of the meat changes, add the soy sauce and wine, blending well. When the juice starts to bubble, remove the mixture and set aside.

Wipe the wok or pan clean with a damp cloth, then heat the remaining oil until smoking. Add the spring onions and bean sprouts, stirring vigorously so every bit of sprout is coated with oil, then add the salt and sugar. Stir for a few more times, then return the pork to the pan and cook for another minute at the very most, stirring constantly. When the bean sprouts start to appear transparent and the juice starts to bubble, the dish is ready. Serve immediately.

Pork Slices with Bamboo Shoots and Chinese Mushrooms

Another name for this delicious dish from Shanghai is Stir-Fried Pork with 'Two Winters': the 'two winters' are winter bamboo shoots and winter mushrooms.

225 g (8 oz) pork fillet
1 tablespoon light soy sauce
1 tablespoon Shao Hsing rice wine or dry sherry
1 tablespoon cornflour mixed with 1 tablespoon cold water
6-8 dried Chinese mushrooms, soaked
225-275 g (8-10 oz) winter bamboo shoots
4 tablespoons oil
1 teaspoon salt
1 teaspoon sugar
½ teaspoon sesame seed oil

Thinly slice the pork and cut into postage-stamp sized pieces. Marinate in a glass bowl with soy sauce, wine and about one-third of the cornflour and water mixture while you prepare the vegetables.

Squeeze dry the mushrooms and discard the hard stalks. Halve or quarter the mushrooms depending on their size. Drain the bamboo shoots and thinly slice the same size as the pork.

Heat the oil in a preheated wok or frying pan until smoking. Stir-fry the pork for about 45 seconds or until the colour changes. Remove with a slotted spoon and set aside. Stir-fry the mushrooms and bamboo shoots, then add the salt and sugar, stirring for about 1 minute. Return the pork to the pan and cook for another minute. Add the remaining cornflour and water mixture and sesame seed oil, blending well. Serve hot.

Rapid-Fried Lamb Slices with Leeks

A very popular dish served in good Peking restaurants. This must be cooked over the highest heat in the shortest possible time.

275-350 g (10-12 oz) leg of lamb fillet
3-4 spring onions
1 tablespoon soy sauce
1 tablespoon Shao Hsing rice wine or dry sherry
2 teaspoons cornflour mixed with a little water
1 teaspoon sesame seed oil
15 g (½ oz) wood ears
1-2 young leeks
600 ml (1 pint) oil for deep-frying
1 clove garlic, crushed
1 teaspoon salt
1 teaspoon sugar
1 tablespoon crushed yellow bean sauce
1 teaspoon vinegar

Trim the excess fat from the lamb and slice as thin as possible. Cut the spring onions in half lengthways, then slice diagonally. Marinate both the lamb and spring onions with soy sauce, wine, cornflour and sesame seed oil for at least 2-3 hours. Meanwhile, soak the wood ears in water for 20-25 minutes, then rinse. Wash the leeks well and cut into small slices.

Heat the oil in a wok or deep-fat fryer until smoking. Stir in the lamb and fry for about 30 seconds, separating the pieces with chopsticks or a carving fork, then quickly remove with a slotted spoon or strainer and drain well on kitchen paper.

Pour off the excess oil, leaving about 2 tablespoons in the wok. Add the garlic, leeks and wood ears, stirring for a few seconds, then add the salt, sugar and bean paste. Stir a few more times, then return the lamb with vinegar and continue stirring about 30 seconds, blending well. Serve hot.

'Ma-Po' Bean Curd (Tofu) with Minced Meat

'Ma-Po' was the wife of a Sichuan chef who worked in the provincial capital Chengdu about one hundred years ago. This universally popular dish has a number of variations, some Cantonese restaurants list it as 'Spicy and Hot Bean Curd' or simply 'Sichuan Bean Curd'.

3 cakes bean curd (tofu)
100 g (4 oz) lean pork, beef or lamb, coarsely chopped
1 leek or 3-4 spring onions
1 tablespoon salted black beans, crushed
1 tablespoon Shao Hsing rice wine or dry sherry
3 tablespoons oil
1 tablespoon chilli bean paste
½ teaspoon salt
1 tablespoon soy sauce
75 ml (3 fl oz) stock (page 24)
2 teaspoons cornflour mixed with a little cold water
ground Sichuan pepper

Cut the bean curd into 1 cm (½ inch) square cubes; blanch them in a pan of boiling water for 2-3 minutes to harden, then drain.

Coarsely chop the meat, cut the leek or spring onions into short lengths and crush the salted black beans, then mix with wine.

Heat the oil in a preheated wok or frying pan until warm, then add the meat and stir-fry until the colour changes. Add chilli bean paste and crushed black beans, reducing the heat for a short time if necessary. Continue stirring and when you can smell the chilli, add the bean curd, salt, soy sauce and stock, then cook for about 3 minutes. Add the leek or spring onions and stir very gently to make sure that the bean curd cubes are not stuck to the bottom of the wok or pan. Blend well, then add the cornflour and water mixture to thicken the sauce.

Serve hot with ground Sichuan pepper.

'Fish Flavoured' Aubergines

This is a popular dish from Sichuan, where it is called *Yu-xiang* (meaning 'fish fragrant' or 'fish sauce') Aubergines. The interesting point is that no fish is used in the recipe – the seasonings for the sauce are exactly the same as for cooking a fish dish, hence the rather misleading name.

175 g (6 oz) lean pork
500 g (1 lb) aubergine
3-4 dried red chillies, soaked in warm water for about 10 minutes
600 ml (1 pint) oil for deep-frying
2 cloves garlic, crushed and finely chopped
3-4 spring onions, finely chopped with white and green parts separated
1 teaspoon finely chopped peeled fresh root ginger
1 tablespoon soy sauce
1 teaspoon sugar
2 tablespoons chilli bean sauce
2 tablespoons Shao Hsing rice wine or dry sherry
2 teaspoons vinegar
2 teaspoons cornflour mixed with 1 tablespoon cold water
1 teaspoon sesame seed oil (optional)

Thinly shred the pork. Discard the aubergine stalks, then cut into diamond-shaped chunks. (You can either peel the aubergine or leave the skin on, as you wish.)

Cut the soaked chillies into 2-3 small bits, discarding the stalks and seeds.

Heat the oil in a preheated wok or deep-fat fryer until smoking. Deep-fry the aubergines for about 3-4 minutes until limp, then remove with a slotted spoon and drain on kitchen paper.

Pour off the excess oil, leaving about 1 tablespoon in the wok. Add the chilli, garlic, spring onion white parts, and ginger to flavour the oil. Add the pork and stir-fry for a few seconds or until the colour of the meat changes from pink to pale white. Add all the seasonings, then the aubergines, blending well together and cook for about 1 minute, stirring constantly. Finally, thicken the sauce with the cornflour and water mixture, add the spring onion green parts and sesame seed oil.

Serve hot.

Note: For vegetarians, leave the pork out of this dish; it will taste just as good.

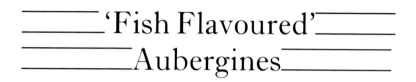

Rapid-Fried Lamb Slices with Leeks.

Mu-Shu Pork with Eggs

Mu-shu is Chinese for a bright yellow flower, and this northern Chinese dish was given the name for its colour. Traditionally it is used as a filling wrapped in thin pancakes, but it can also be wrapped inside a crisp Webb's or iceberg lettuce leaves, or just served on its own.

15 g (½ oz) wood ears
175-225 g (6-8 oz) pork fillet or steak
100 g (4 oz) bamboo shoots
225 g (8 oz) cabbage or leeks
3-4 eggs, or 2 eggs plus any extra yolks from the egg whites used for other seafood or chicken dishes
1 teaspoon salt
4 tablespoons oil
2 spring onions, thinly shredded
1 tablespoon light soy sauce
1 tablespoon Shao Hsing rice wine or dry sherry
1 teaspoon sesame seed oil

Soak the wood ears for approximately 25 minutes, then rinse and thinly shred.

Shred the pork into matchstick-sized pieces.

Cut the bamboo shoots into matchstick-sized pieces. Shred the cabbage so it resembles fine coleslaw.

Lightly beat the eggs with your chopsticks and add a pinch of salt.

Heat about 1 tablespoon oil in a preheated wok or frying pan, then reduce the heat and scramble the eggs until set. Remove and set on one side.

Increase the heat to high again and heat the remaining oil until smoking.

Stir-fry the pork for 30-40 seconds or until the colour changes, then add the cabbage, bamboo shoots, wood ears and spring onions, stirring for about 30 seconds.

Add the salt, soy sauce and wine.

Continue stirring for 1-1½ minutes, then add the scrambled eggs, stirring to break the eggs into shreds and to mix all the ingredients together thoroughly.

When all the ingredients are well blended together, add the sesame seed oil as a garnish.

Serve immediately.

Fish Fillet in Wine Sauce, Peking Style

Traditionally, very fragrant fermented rice grains are used to flavour this dish; I find a little brandy or whisky has almost the same effect.

25 g (1 oz) wood ears
450 g (1 lb) fillet of any flat fish, such as plaice or sole
1 egg white, lightly beaten
2 tablespoons cornflour mixed with 3 tablespoons water
600 ml (1 pint) oil for deep-frying
1-2 cloves garlic, crushed and finely chopped
1½ teaspoons salt
1 teaspoon sugar
50 ml (2 fl oz) stock (page 24)
4 tablespoons Shao Hsing rice wine or dry sherry
1-2 tablespoons brandy or whisky
1 teaspoon sesame seed oil

Soak the wood ears in water for 20-25 minutes. Pat the fish dry and leave the skin on. Cut into fairly large pieces and mix with egg white and about half of the cornflour. Rinse and clean the wood ears, discarding any hard bits.

Heat the oil in a preheated wok or deep-fat fryer until fairly hot, then reduce heat and let the oil cool down a little before adding the fish, piece by piece, and frying for about 1 minute. Separate the pieces and turn them over very gently with a pair of chopsticks or tongs. Remove with a slotted spoon or strainer and drain on kitchen paper.

Pour off the excess oil, leaving about 1 tablespoon in the wok. Increase the heat to high again, add the crushed garlic, wood ears, salt, sugar and the stock. Return to the boil, then return the fish with wine and brandy or whisky. When the sauce starts to boil again, add the remaining cornflour and water mixture very slowly, tilting the wok to distribute it evenly. As soon as the sauce thickens, garnish with sesame seed oil and serve hot.

66

Left to right: Fish Fillet in Wine Sauce, Peking Style; Sichuan Prawns with Garlic and Chilli Sauce; Quick-Fried Seafood with Vegetables.

Sichuan Prawns with Garlic and Chilli Sauce

Again, try to get uncooked prawns in their shells; if using ready cooked ones, then there is no need to deep-fry first before braising them in the delicious sauce.

225-275 g (8-10 oz) headless king prawns, defrosted if frozen
600 ml (1 pint) oil for deep-frying
3-4 dried red chillies, soaked in warm water for about 10 minutes and finely chopped
1 clove garlic, finely chopped
½ teaspoon finely chopped peeled fresh root ginger
1 tablespoon light or dark soy sauce
1 tablespoon Shao Hsing rice wine or dry sherry
1 tablespoon chilli bean sauce
1 teaspoon tomato purée
3 tablespoons stock (page 24) or water
2 spring onions, finely chopped
2 teaspoons cornflour mixed with 1 tablespoon water
a few drops of sesame seed oil
lettuce leaves, to garnish

Wash and dry the prawns with kitchen paper. Remove the legs and tails by pulling them off with your fingers, but leave the body shells on. Using a sharp knife or a pair of kitchen scissors, cut a slit along the back shell, then carefully remove the vein and cut each prawn into 2 or 3 pieces.

Heat the oil in a preheated wok or deep-fat fryer. Fry the prawns for 35-40 seconds or until they turn bright pink. Quickly remove with a slotted spoon or strainer and drain on kitchen paper.

Pour off the excess oil, leaving about 1 tablespoon in the wok, then add the chillies, garlic, ginger, soy sauce, wine, chilli bean paste, tomato purée and stock or water and braise the prawns over moderate heat for about 1½ minutes, stirring constantly. Add the finely chopped spring onions and thicken the sauce with the cornflour and water mixture. Add the sesame seed oil and serve on a bed of lettuce leaves.

Quick-Fried Seafood with Vegetables

This is a very colourful and delicious dish from Canton. You can either use one of the two shellfish, or both together.

4-6 fresh scallops
100-175 g (4-6 oz) uncooked prawns
½ egg white, lightly beaten
1 tablespoon cornflour mixed with a little water
2-3 celery stalks
1 red pepper, cored and seeded
1-2 carrots
600 ml (1 pint) oil for deep-frying
1 teaspoon finely chopped peeled fresh root ginger
2 spring onions, finely chopped
1 teaspoon salt
2 tablespoons Shao Hsing rice wine or dry sherry
1 tablespoon light soy sauce
1-2 teaspoons chilli bean sauce (optional)
a little stock or water (optional)
a few drops of sesame seed oil

Cut each scallop into 3-4 slices. Shell the prawns and, depending on their size, leave them whole if small, or cut each into 2-3 pieces. Mix the seafood with the egg white and about half of the cornflour and water mixture.

Slice the celery, red pepper and carrots into pieces roughly the same size and shape as a postage stamp.

Heat the oil in a preheated wok or deep-fat fryer until fairly hot, then reduce heat and let the oil cool down a little before adding the seafood. Stir to separate the pieces, then cook for 30 seconds at most. Remove with a slotted spoon or strainer and drain on kitchen paper.

Pour off the excess oil, leaving about 2 tablespoons in the wok. Increase heat to high again and add the ginger and spring onions to flavour the oil for a few seconds, then add the vegetables. Stir-fry for about 1 minute, then return the seafood to the wok. Add the salt, wine, soy sauce and chilli bean paste (if using). Stir a few more times, then add a little stock or water *only* if it is necessary.

Finally, add the remaining cornflour and water mixture to thicken the gravy and blend everything together well. Add the sesame seed oil and serve hot.

Broccoli in Oyster Sauce

Also known as calabrese, broccoli has the subtle, fresh texture of cauliflower with the delicate succulence of asparagus. The Cantonese are particularly fond of the crunchy stalks, and oyster sauce seems to have made an ideal partner for this vegetable.

500 g (1 lb) fresh broccoli
3-4 tablespoons oil
2-3 small pieces peeled fresh root ginger
1 teaspoon salt
1 teaspoon sugar
2-3 tablespoons stock (page 24) or water
2 tablespoons oyster sauce

Cut the broccoli heads into florets, removing the rough skin from the stalks, then diagonally slice them into diamond-shaped chunks.

Heat the oil in a preheated wok or frying pan until smoking. Add the ginger to flavour the oil for a few seconds, then add the broccoli and stir-fry for about 1 minute. Add the salt and sugar and continue stirring, then add the stock or water to quick-braise the vegetable. Finally, add the oyster sauce and blend well. Serve hot or cold.

Fillet of Sole with Mushrooms

This is my version of the French Filets de Sole Bonne Femme, but I am sure you will agree that my method is much simpler – and, dare I say, perhaps even more delicious?

350-400 g (12-14 oz) fillet of sole
1 egg white, lightly beaten
1 tablespoon cornflour mixed with 1 tablespoon cold water
175 g (6 oz) fresh mushrooms
600 ml (1 pint) oil for deep-frying
2 spring onions, cut into short lengths
1-2 slices peeled fresh root ginger, finely shredded
1 teaspoon salt
1 teaspoon sugar
1 tablespoon light soy sauce
1 tablespoon Shao Hsing rice wine or dry sherry
125 ml (4 fl oz) stock (page 24)
a few drops of sesame seed oil, to garnish

Pat dry the fillets and trim off the soft bones along the edges. Depending on their size, leave the fillets whole if small, otherwise cut the fish into half if big. Gently mix together with the egg white and cornflour mixture. Wash and thinly slice the mushrooms without peeling.

Heat the oil in a preheated wok or deep-fat fryer until smoking, then reduce heat and let the oil cool down a little before adding the fish and frying for 1½-2 minutes or until golden and crisp. Remove and drain well on kitchen paper.

Pour off the excess oil, leaving about 2 tablespoons in the wok. Increase the heat to high again, then add the spring onions, ginger, and mushrooms, stirring for about 30 seconds. Add the salt, sugar, soy sauce and wine and continue stirring for a few more times. Add the stock and bring to the boil. Return the fish to the sauce and braise for about 1 minute. Finally, add the sesame seed oil and serve hot.

Fillet of Sole with Mushrooms (top); Fish Steak in Sweet and Sour Sauce (bottom).

Fish Steak in Sweet and Sour Sauce

For best result, use small cutlets from the tail end of the fish.

500 g (1 lb) fish cutlets, such as cod, haddock or monkfish
1 egg, lightly beaten
2-3 tablespoons cornflour mixed with 2-3 tablespoons water
600 ml (1 pint) oil for deep-frying

Sauce:
1½ tablespoons sugar
1 tablespoon soy sauce
1 tablespoon Shao Hsing rice wine or dry sherry
1 tablespoon vinegar
1-2 spring onions, finely chopped
1 teaspoon finely chopped peeled fresh root ginger
50 ml (2 fl oz) stock (page 24) or water
1 tablespoon cornflour mixed with 1 tablespoon water

Dry the fish well and keep the skin on or they will fall apart during cooking. Blend the beaten egg with the cornflour and water mixture to make a light batter.

Heat the oil in a preheated wok or deep-fat fryer until smoking. Reduce the heat and let the oil cool down a little. Dip the fish cutlets in the batter and turn to coat well. Slide the cutlets into the oil, one by one, and stir very gently to separate them. Increase the heat to high again and fry for about 2 minutes or until the fish turn golden brown. Remove with a slotted spoon or strainer and drain.

Pour off excess oil, leaving about 1 tablespoon in the wok. Mix all the sauce ingredients together and add to the wok, stirring until thickened. Return the fish, blend well and cook for about 1 minute at most, gently stirring constantly. Serve hot.

'Crab' with Egg White

In China, crabs are highly prized, particularly in the north since they are less abundant there than in southern China. That's why, as in this recipe, certain types of fish are made to resemble a 'crab' flavour.

500 g (1 lb) fillets of richly flavoured fish, such as haddock
1½ tablespoons cornflour
4 egg whites, lightly beaten
600 ml (1 pint) oil for deep-frying
3 tablespoons chicken stock
1 teaspoon salt
1 teaspoon finely chopped peeled fresh root ginger
1 tablespoon Shao Hsing rice wine or dry sherry
2 teaspoons vinegar
2 egg yolks

Skin and bone the fish before thinly shredding. Sprinkle with the cornflour, then mix with the egg whites.

Heat the oil in a very hot wok or deep-fat fryer until warm. Stir in the fish shreds and fry for about 1 minute, then remove with a slotted spoon or strainer and drain on kitchen paper.

Pour off the excess oil, add the stock, salt and ginger and return to the boil. Return the fish to the wok with the wine and vinegar, stirring gently for about 1 minute.

Place the fish on a serving dish with the raw egg yolks on top. Bring to the table, then break the yolks and stir into the fish just before serving.

Egg Fu-Yung
with Prawns or Crab

Strictly speaking, *fu-yung* should be lightly scrambled egg-whites with a creamy texture; in most Chinese restaurants, however, a *fu-yung* dish usually means an omelet. (See also Chicken Fu-Yung, page 51.)

5-6 eggs
100 g (4 oz) peeled prawns, defrosted if frozen, or flaked crab meat, drained if canned
½ teaspoon finely chopped peeled fresh root ginger
2 spring onions, finely chopped
1 teaspoon salt
100 g (4 oz) bamboo shoots, or 50 g (2 oz) button mushrooms
3-4 tablespoons oil
1 tablespoon Shao Hsing rice wine or dry sherry
coriander leaves or parsley, to garnish

Lightly beat the eggs together, then add the prawns or crab meat, ginger, about one-third of the spring onions and a pinch of salt. Thinly slice the bamboo shoots or mushrooms.

Heat the oil in a preheated wok or frying pan until smoking. Add the remaining spring onions and bamboo shoots or mushrooms and stir for about 30 seconds, then add the salt and wine, stir a few times more. Pour in the eggs. Reduce the heat and stir to scramble until set, but not too hard.

Serve hot, garnished with coriander leaves or parsley.

Quick Fried 'Crystal'
Prawns

For best results, use headless, uncooked and unshelled prawns, ideally about 5cm (2 inches) long.

500 g (1 lb) headless king prawns, defrosted if frozen
1 egg white, lightly beaten
1 tablespoon cornflour mixed with 1 tablespoon cold water
600 ml (1 pint) oil for deep-frying
1 teaspoon finely chopped peeled fresh root ginger
2 spring onions, white parts only, finely chopped
1½ teaspoons salt
1 tablespoon Shao Hsing rice wine or dry sherry
2-3 tablespoons chicken stock

Shell and devein the prawns, then wash under cold running water for at least 10-15 minutes or until the water is clean. Dry thoroughly with kitchen paper. Mix with the egg white, then the cornflour and water mixture, blending well with your fingers. Cover and refrigerate for about 3 hours.

Heat the oil in a very hot wok until warm. Add the prawns and separate them with chopsticks. Remove after 20-25 seconds with slotted spoon or strainer and drain on kitchen paper.

Pour off the excess oil and return the prawns to the wok with the ginger, spring onions, salt and wine. Stir and toss for about 30 seconds, then add the stock, and continue stirring for 1 minute at most. Be careful not to overcook.

The prawns should look bright white like crystal, and taste delicious and tender, almost melting in your mouth.

Serve immediately.

Squid-Flowers
with Green Peppers

This is another recipe from the Cantonese school of cuisine, and one of their specialities is seafood cooking.

450 g (1 lb) squid
1 large or 2 small green peppers, cored and seeded
3-4 tablespoons oil
1 clove garlic, crushed and finely chopped
1 teaspoon finely chopped peeled fresh root ginger
1-2 spring onions, finely chopped
1 teaspoon salt
2 teaspoons vinegar
1 tablespoon Shao Hsing rice wine or dry sherry
1 tablespoon salted black bean sauce
a few drops sesame seed oil
coriander leaves, to garnish

Clean the squid by discarding the head and the transparent backbone as well as the ink bag; peel off the thin skin, then wash and dry. Open up the squid and score the *inside* in a criss-cross pattern, then cut into pieces about the size of an oblong postage stamp. Blanch in a pan of boiling water; each piece will curl up and the criss-cross pattern will open out to resemble ears of corn – hence the name of 'squid-flower' for this dish.

Cut the green peppers into triangular pieces about the size of a postage stamp.

Heat the oil in a very hot wok or frying pan until smoking. Add

the garlic, ginger, spring onions, green peppers and squid and stir-fry for about 30 seconds. Add the salt, vinegar, wine and black bean sauce and continue stirring for another minute to blend well. Finally add the sesame seed oil and serve hot with coriander leaves.

Note: Overcooking will make the squid tough.

Rapid-Fried Prawns in Sweet and Sour Sauce

Squid Flowers with Green Peppers (left); Quick-Fried 'Crystal' Prawns (right).

This recipe originated in Shanghai and you will find it quite different from the Cantonese version; no gluey tomato ketchup or bits of pineapple are used. The result is a very delicate and delicious dish with the subtle sweet and sour taste.

25 g (1 oz) wood ears
225 g (8 oz) uncooked prawns, defrosted if frozen
1 teaspoon salt
½ egg white, lightly beaten
2 teaspoons cornflour mixed with 1 tablespoon water
100 g (4 oz) canned water chestnuts
3-4 tablespoons oil
½ teaspoon finely chopped peeled fresh root ginger
2 spring onions, finely chopped
1 tablespoon light soy sauce
1 tablespoon sugar
1 tablespoon vinegar
1 tablespoon Shao Hsing rice wine or dry sherry
about 2 tablespoons stock (page 24) or water

Soak the wood ears in water for 20-25 minutes then rinse and discard any hard bits at the root.

Shell and devein the prawns, then dry. Slit each prawn in half lengthways if large or leave whole if small; select prawns roughly the same size because it will not do to have a mixture of different sizes and shapes in the same dish.

Mix the prawns with a pinch of salt, the egg white and the cornflour mixture, blending well with your fingers.

Drain the water chestnuts and cut into slices.

Heat the oil in a very hot wok or frying pan to moderate, then reduce the heat to low and let the oil cool down a little before stir-frying the prawns for about 15-20 seconds. Quickly scoop out with a slotted spoon and set aside. (Needless to say, if using cooked prawns, this first stage of stir-frying can be omitted.)

Increase the heat to high again and wait for the oil to smoke.

Add the ginger and spring onions and fry for a few seconds to flavour the oil, then add the wood ears, water chestnuts and prepared prawns. Stir for about 30 seconds, then add the soy sauce, sugar, vinegar, wine and the stock or water. Continue stirring for another 1 minute at most.

Serve immediately the sauce starts to bubble and everything is well blended.

It makes my mouth water just to think about this dish!

Rice, Noodles and Snacks

Traditionally, rice has been the staple food for people south of the Yangtze River, while people in north China had to rely far more on wheat products for their everyday meals. But with the advancement of technology for cultivation, plus much improved transportation, it is almost true to say that plain boiled or steamed rice is the bulk food for the Chinese both in the north and south, while fried rice or noodles (fried or in soup) are often served on their own as a light meal or snack. The Chinese do not have much 'bread' in the Western sense, but we do eat steamed buns, dumplings and pancakes, both sweet and savoury.

The Chinese seldom conclude an everyday meal with a dessert. Most sweet dishes are served either as a snack or, on more formal occasions, served between courses to cleanse the palate, in the same manner as a sorbet in the West.

Singapore-Style Fried 'Rice Sticks'

Also known as rice noodles or vermicelli, rice sticks are very popular in southern China, where they are interchangeable with noodles made from wheat flour in most recipes.

275-350 g (10-12 oz) rice noodles
1 tablespoon dried shrimps, soaked
100 g (4 oz) lean pork or beef
1 medium onion
100 g (4 oz) fresh bean sprouts
1 leek or 2 spring onions
4 tablespoons oil
1 teaspoon salt
2 teaspoons curry powder
2 tablespoons light soy sauce
1 green or red chilli, seeded and thinly shredded (optional)

Soak the rice noodles in hot water for 10-15 minutes or until soft, then drain, rinse in cold water and drain again.

Drain the dried shrimps and rinse.

Coarsely chop the meat, thinly slice the onion, rinse the bean sprouts and cut the leek or spring onions into thin shreds.

Heat about 2 tablespoons oil in a preheated wok or frying pan until hot, then add the meat and stir to separate each piece. As soon as the colour of the meat changes, add the onion, leek or spring onions, shrimps, bean sprouts, salt and curry powder, then cook for about 2 minutes. Remove and reserve as 'dressing'.

Add the remaining oil, wait for it to smoke, then add the drained rice noodles and stir to make sure that each 'stick' is covered with oil. Add the soy sauce, the 'dressing' and, if using, the chilli shreds. Stir and toss well for about 1 minute or until well blended. Serve hot or cold.

Yangchow Fried Rice

Yangchow cuisine from the Yangtze River delta occupies a particularly important position in the development of Chinese cookery. Apart from the well known Lions' Heads and 'Squirrel' Fish, and many noodle dishes, several of the Cantonese *dim sums* are of Yangchow origin.

There are at least a dozen variations of 'fried rice' – from simple Egg fried rice to the special Ten-variety fried rice: besides the basic ingredient of rice, other items such as egg, shrimps, ham, pork, chicken, giblets, mushrooms, bamboo shoots and green peas, etc., can be added singly or in various combinations as desired.

The rice to be used for frying should not be too hard or too soft; ideally it should be soaked in water for a short while before cooking.

This will serve 4-6 as a light meal or snack when served with one or two other dishes; or will serve 10-12 as part of a buffet or dinner party when there are a number or other dishes.

3-4 dried Chinese mushrooms, soaked
100 g (4 oz) cooked chicken meat, ham, or pork (Cha Shao Roast Pork, page 33, or Crispy Roast Pork, page 30, or Fragrant Pork, page 21)
100 g (4 oz) bamboo shoots
4 eggs
1½ teaspoons salt
2 spring onions, finely chopped
4 tablespoons oil
100 g (4 oz) peeled prawns
100 g (4 oz) green peas
2 tablespoons Shao Hsing rice wine or dry sherry
1 tablespoon light soy sauce
450 g (1 lb) cooked rice

Squeeze the mushrooms dry and discard the stalks.

Cut into dice the mushrooms, chicken, ham or pork and bamboo shoots about the same size as the prawns or peas.

Lightly beat the eggs with a pinch of salt and a few bits of finely chopped spring onions; set aside.

Heat about 2 tablespoons oil in a very hot wok or frying pan and stir-fry the diced mushrooms, chicken, ham or pork, bamboo shoots, prawns and peas.

Add the wine and soy sauce, stir all the ingredients together for about 2 minutes, then remove from the wok, set aside and keep warm as 'dressing'.

Heat the remaining oil and lightly scramble the beaten eggs. Add the cooked rice, remaining spring onions and salt; stir to make sure that each grain of rice is separated, then add about half of the 'dressing' and blend well. Carefully place the remaining 'dressing' on top as a garnish.

Serve immediately.

Yangchow Fried Rice

Plain Boiled Rice

In the Chinese language, there is a distinction between raw rice *(mi)* and cooked rice *(fan)*. In everyday usage, the Chinese word for 'cooked rice' and 'staple food' are synonymous, just as in English the word 'bread' is used in 'give us our daily bread' or 'bread-winner'.

There are two main types of rice on sale in the West: the long grain or patna rice, and the rounded or pudding rice. If you like your rice to be firm yet fluffy, then use the long grain type, as the rounded rice tends to be rather soft and sticks together when cooked. Allow 50 g (2 oz) raw rice per person, unless you are very hearty eaters.

350 g (12 oz) rice
400-450 ml (14-16 fl oz) cold water
½ teaspoon salt

Wash and rinse the rice in cold water just once. Place the rice in a saucepan and cover with about 2.5 cm (1 inch) water. Bring to the boil, then add salt and give the rice a stir to prevent it sticking to the bottom of the pan.

Reduce the heat to very, very low, cover with a tight-fitting lid and cook for 15-20 minutes. Remove from the heat and let stand for 10 minutes or so, then fluff up the rice with a fork or spoon.

Wonton and Noodle Soup

When wontons are served in a clear broth in China, it is meant to be a snack rather than a soup, and when wontons are cooked with noodles, the dish becomes a substantial main course.

100 g (4 oz) leafy green vegetable, such as spinach or cabbage
175 g (6 oz) pork, not too lean, coarsely chopped
½ teaspoon salt
1 teaspoon sugar
2 teaspoons light soy sauce
1 tablespoon Shao Hsing rice wine or dry sherry
2 spring onions, finely chopped
1 teaspoon sesame seed oil
24 ready-made wonton skins
225 g (8 oz) dried, or 350 g (12 oz) fresh egg noodles
850 ml (1½ pints) Clear Soup (page 24) or chicken broth
soy sauce, finely chopped spring onions and sesame seed oil, to garnish

Blanch the vegetable until soft, then drain and coarsely chop. Mix with the pork, salt, sugar, soy sauce, wine, spring onions and sesame seed oil. Blend thoroughly together to make a smooth mixture for the filling.

To make the wontons, place about 1 teaspoon filling in the centre of a wonton skin. Bring the opposite corners together in a fold and seal by pinching the top edges together firmly. Fold the other two corners towards each other and seal.

Cook the noodles according to the instructions on the packet. Drain, rinse under cold water, then place in a large serving bowl. Meanwhile, bring the stock or broth to a rolling boil, drop in the wontons and boil rapidly for 2-3 minutes. Pour into the serving bowl over the noodles and garnish with soy sauce, spring onions and sesame seed oil. Serve hot.

Additional ingredients such as thinly shredded chicken or pork, and bamboo shoots, as well as green vegetables are often added to the 'soup'. Also, the filling can have additional ingredients, such as prawns or mushrooms.

Deep-Fried Wontons

The highly popular crispy wontons served with sweet and sour sauce (often full of tomato ketchup) in some Cantonese restaurants are, like *crispy fried noodles* and *chop suey*, purely a Western innovation.

Fresh or frozen ready-made wonton skins are available from Oriental stores. It is simply a matter of wrapping the filling, cooking and making the sauce.

100 g (4 oz) lean pork, coarsely chopped
50 g (2 oz) fatty pork, finely chopped
50 g (2 oz) peeled prawns, finely chopped
2 teaspoons light soy sauce
1 teaspoon sugar
1 tablespoon Shao Hsing rice wine or dry sherry
2 teaspoons finely chopped spring onions
24 ready-made wonton skins
1 litre (1¾ pints) oil for deep-frying

Sauce:

1 tablespoon oil
1 tablespoon sugar
2 tablespoons vinegar
1 tablespoon light soy sauce
1 tablespoon tomato purée (do not use tomato ketchup)
2 teaspoons cornflour mixed with 2-3 tablespoons water

Mix the pork and prawns with soy sauce, sugar, wine and spring onions. Blend well and leave to stand for 25-30 minutes.

Place about 1 teaspoon filling at the centre of a wonton skin, fold over from corner to corner, wetting a small part of the skin on the sides immediately around the filling, then press securely together.

Heat the oil in a preheated wok or deep-fat-fryer until smoking, then turn down the heat to let the oil cool a little before deep-frying the wontons in batches for 2-3 minutes, or until crispy. Remove and drain well on kitchen paper.

To keep the wontons warm and crispy until ready to serve, place them on a baking sheet lined with kitchen paper in a preheated 150C/300F/Gas 2 oven.

To make the sauce, heat the oil in a preheated wok or saucepan, then reduce heat and add the sugar, vinegar, soy sauce and tomato purée. Stir to blend well, then add the cornflour and water mixture to make a smooth sauce. Serve immediately with the wontons while both are hot.

Noodles in Soup

In China, noodles in soup *(tang mein)* are far more commonly served than *chow mein*. This recipe again is a basic one; you can use different items for the 'dressing' to suit your preference or according to what is available.

225 g (8 oz) chicken breast meat, beef steak or pork fillet, or 100 g
(4 oz) cooked meat such as Cha Shao (page 33), or 'White-Cut'
Chicken (page 22)
1 teaspoon cornflour
4-6 dried Chinese mushrooms, soaked
100 g (4 oz) bamboo shoots
100 g (4 oz) spinach leaves, lettuce, or Chinese cabbage
2 spring onions, thinly shredded
350 g (12 oz) dried egg noodles or vermicelli
600 ml (1 pint) chicken or meat stock
3 tablespoons oil
1 teaspoon salt
1 teaspoon sugar
2 tablespoons light soy sauce
1 tablespoon Shao Hsing rice wine or dry sherry
1 teaspoon sesame seed oil, to garnish

Thinly shred the meat (use one kind only) and coat with cornflour mixed with a little water. If using cooked meat, you can mix pork with chicken if you like (but not pork with beef), but cooked meat shouldn't be cut too fine, or coated with cornflour.

Squeeze dry the mushrooms and discard the stalks. Thinly shred the mushrooms, bamboo shoots, spinach and spring onions.

Cook the noodles in boiling water according to the instructions on the packet, then drain and rinse under cold water. Place in a large serving bowl. Bring the stock to a boil and pour over the noodles; keep warm.

Heat the oil in a preheated hot wok or frying pan until smoking. Add about half of the spring onions to flavour the oil for 1-2 seconds, then add the uncooked meat and stir to separate the shreds. As soon as the colour of the meat changes, add the mushrooms, bamboo shoots and spinach. Stir for about 1 minute, then add salt, sugar, soy sauce and wine and continue stirring until well blended. Pour this 'dressing' over the noodles. Garnish with the remaining spring onions and sesame seed oil. Serve hot.

Deep-Fried Wontons with Sweet and Sour Sauce (left); Noodles in Soup (right).

Red Bean Paste Pancakes

These pancakes, when unfilled, are traditionally served with dishes such as Peking Duck (page 42) or *Mu-shu* pork. But, of course, you can use them as a wrapper for any dish instead of serving rice with it. The pancakes can be made well in advance and can be frozen, unfilled, then warmed by steaming for 5 minutes before use.

Thin pancakes:
500 g (1 lb) plain flour
275 ml (½ pint) boiling water
1 teaspoon oil

Sift the flour into a mixing bowl, then very gently pour in the water mixed with oil, stirring as you pour.

Knead the mixture into a firm dough. Cover with a damp towel and set aside for about 30 minutes. Lightly dust a work surface with flour, knead the dough for 5-8 minutes or until smooth, then divide it into 3 equal portions. Roll out each portion into a long 'sausage' and cut each into 8-10 pieces. Using the palm of your hand, press each piece into a flat pancake. Dust the surface with more flour, flatten each pancake into a 15 cm (6 inch) circle with a rolling pin, and roll gently on both sides.

Place an ungreased frying pan over high heat. When hot, reduce the heat to low and depending on the size of the frying pan, place 1-3 pancakes at a time in the pan. Turn over when little brown spots appear on the underside. Remove and keep under a damp cloth until you have finished making all 24-30 pancakes.

Red Bean Paste Pancakes:

Sweetened chestnut purée can be used as a substitute for red bean paste.

100 g (4 oz) sweetened red bean paste
6 thin pancakes (see above)
3 tablespoons oil
1 teaspoon sugar

Spread about 1 tablespoon red bean paste over about four-fifths of the pancake surface, and roll it over three or four times to form a flattened roll.

Heat the oil in a frying pan and shallow-fry the pancakes until golden brown, turning over once.

Cut each pancake roll into 3-4 pieces, sprinkle over the sugar and serve hot.

Peking Dumplings

500 g (1 lb) plain flour
275 ml (½ pint) water

Filling
450 g (1 lb) Chinese cabbage
225 g (8 oz) pork, beef or lamb, minced
4 spring onions, finely chopped
1-2 teaspoons finely chopped fresh root ginger
1 tablespoon light soy sauce
1 tablespoon Shao Hsing rice wine or dry sherry
½ teaspoon salt
1 teaspoon sugar
1 teaspoon sesame seed oil
2.5 litres (4½ pints) water
soy sauce and vinegar mixed for dipping sauce

Sift the flour into a mixing bowl, slowly pour in the water and mix to a firm dough. Knead in the bowl until smooth and soft, then cover with a damp cloth and set aside for about 30 minutes.

To make the filling, blanch the cabbage leaves until soft, then drain and finely chop. Mix with the minced meat, spring onion, ginger, soy sauce, wine, salt, sugar and sesame seed oil. Blend together thoroughly.

Lightly dust a work surface with flour, and knead and roll the dough into a long sausage about 5 cm (2 inches) in diameter. Cut it into 60 small pieces. Flatten each piece with the palm of your hand, then use a rolling pin to roll out each piece into a pancake about 7.5 cm (3 inches) in diameter.

To make the dumplings, place 2 teaspoons filling in the centre of each pancake and fold the dough into a half-moon-shaped pouch, then pinch the edges firmly so that the dumpling is tightly sealed.

Bring the water to a rolling boil in a large pot or pan over high heat. Drop in about 20 dumplings, one by one, stirring gently with chopsticks or a long-handled spoon to prevent them sticking together. When the water starts to boil again, add about 125 ml (4 fl oz) cold water to the pot; return to the boil and add more cold water. Repeat this process 3 or 4 times, then the dumplings will be done. Remove with a strainer or slotted spoon and serve hot with the dipping sauce.

Uncooked dumplings can be frozen, then boiled, steamed or shallow-fried from frozen. Shallow-fried dumplings are also known as *guotie*, which literally means 'pan-stuck' or 'pot-sticker' – they should be crispy on the bottom, soft on the top and juicy inside.

Chow Mein

This is a basic *chow mein* recipe, and the 'dressing' can be any of the items that happen to be around. Only bear in mind the principle of cutting all ingredients into matching shapes and sizes for the same dish: all the ingredients should be cut into thin shreds for a noodle dish.

275 g (20 oz) dried, or 450 g (1 lb) fresh egg noodles, or spaghetti or tagliatelle
225 g (8 oz) chicken breast meat, beef steak, or pork fillet, etc., or 100 g (4 oz) cooked meat, such as Chao Shao (page 33), or Crispy Roast Pork (page 30)
4-5 tablespoons oil
2 spring onions, thinly shredded
100 g (4 oz) mange-tout or French beans
100 g (4 oz) peeled prawns (optional)
1 teaspoon salt
1-2 tablespoons Shao Hsing rice wine
2 tablespoons light soy sauce
1 teaspoon sesame seed oil, to garnish

Cook the noodles in boiling water according to the instructions on the packet, then drain and rinse under cold water until cool; set aside. Fresh noodles require far less cooking time; they usually only need to be soaked in boiling water for 1-2 minutes before rinsing in cold water.

Thinly shred the meat. Do not use more than one type for the same dish – do not mix chicken with beef, or beef with pork.

Heat about 2 tablespoons oil in a preheated wok or frying pan until hot, then add about half the spring onions, meat, vegetable and prawns. Stir for about 1 minute, then add salt and wine and continue stirring for 1 minute. Remove and keep warm as the 'dressing'.

Heat the remaining oil, add the remaining spring onions and the noodles, then stir for about 1 minute. Add about half of the 'dressing' and soy sauce and stir about 1 more minute until well blended and thoroughly heated through. Remove to a large serving dish, pour the remaining 'dressing' on top and garnish with sesame seed oil. Serve hot or cold.

Chow Mein.

Spring Rolls

This is a Shanghai recipe; these spring rolls are small and dainty, and do not contain the ubiquitous bean sprout.

20 ready-made spring roll skins
225 g (8 oz) pork fillet or chicken breast meat
1 tablespoon light soy sauce
1 tablespoon Shao Hsing rice wine or dry sherry
1 teaspoon cornflour
5-6 dried Chinese mushrooms, soaked
100 g (4 oz) bamboo shoots or young carrots
225 g (8 oz) young tender leeks or spring onions
3 tablespoons oil
1 teaspoon salt
1 teaspoon sugar
2 teaspoons plain flour mixed with a little water
extra flour for dusting
1 litre (1¾ pints) oil for deep-frying

Take the spring roll skins out of the packet and defrost thoroughly. Cover with a damp cloth to prevent them getting too dry and hard, while you make the filling.

Thinly shred the pork or chicken. Blend together the soy sauce, wine and cornflour, then add the meat to marinate while you prepare the vegetables. Squeeze the mushrooms dry and discard the stalks. Cut the mushrooms, bamboo shoots or carrots, and leeks or spring onions all into thin shreds.

Heat the oil in a preheated wok or frying pan until smoking, add the meat first, stir to separate the shreds, then add the vegetables. Stir-fry for about 1 minute, then add salt and sugar and continue stirring for another minute or so. Add a little stock or water *only* if necessary. Remove from the heat and set aside to cool for at least 30 minutes.

Make the spring rolls: cut a square sheet of spring roll skin in half diagonally to make two triangles. Place about 2 teaspoons of the filling on the skin about one-third of the way down. With the triangle pointing away from you, lift the lower flap over the filling and roll once, then fold both ends and roll once more. Brush the upper edge with a little flour and water paste, and roll into a neat package.

Lightly dust a tray with flour and place the spring rolls in rows with the flap sides down. They can be kept in the refrigerator for up to 2 days or frozen for up to 3 months.

To cook, heat the oil in a preheated wok or deep-fat fryer until smoking, then turn down the heat a little before deep-frying the spring rolls in batches for 3-4 minutes, or until golden and crispy. Increase the heat to high again before frying next batch, and as each batch is cooked, remove and drain well on kitchen paper. Serve hot with a dipping sauce, such as soy sauce, vinegar or chilli sauce; these are ideal for a buffet or as cocktail snacks.

Peking Toffee Apples

The term 'toffee' here should be 'candied floss' – *ba-si* in Chinese, from which the Pekingese name 'Drawn Thread Apple' is derived. Besides apples, banana and sweet potatoes can be prepared and cooked the same way.

4 firm eating apples, peeled and cored
4 tablespoons plain flour
2 tablespoons cold water
1 egg, beaten
1 litre (1¾ pints) oil for deep-frying
100 g (4 oz) granulated sugar
2 teaspoons sesame seeds

Cut each apple into about 8-10 pieces. Sprinkle with a little of the dry flour. Make a batter by mixing the remaining flour and water into a smooth paste, then add the beaten egg and blend well.

Heat the oil in a preheated wok or deep-fat fryer. Coat each piece of apple with the batter, then deep-fry for about 3 minutes or until golden. Remove and drain well on kitchen paper.

Pour off the excess oil, leaving about 1 tablespoon in the wok; reduce the heat to low, add the sugar, stirring constantly until the sugar has caramelized. The secret lies in timing and heat control: the caramelizing happens so quickly and suddenly that it is crucial you do not look away or stop stirring for even a second.

As soon as the sugar has caramelized, add the apple pieces, stir, and add the sesame seeds. Blend well. As soon as each piece of apple is covered by the toffee, dip in cold water to harden before serving. Serve at once.

Note If using bananas, choose firm ones and cut into 2.5-cm (1-inch) pieces. Sweet potatoes should be peeled and cut into 2.5-cm (1-inch) pieces. Sprinkle with flour and proceed as for Toffee Apples.

Chinese Fruit Salad made with lychees, melon, tangerines, strawberries, nectarines, grapes and kiwi fruit.

Chinese Fruit Salad

This is most refreshing, particularly when served at the end of a big meal or banquet. The variety of fresh and canned fruit should consist of a few exotic and colourful items, such as kiwi fruit (also known as Chinese gooseberry), lychees, peaches and so on.

225 g (8 oz) rock candy or crystal sugar (optional)
600 ml (1 pint) boiling water (optional)
1 small watermelon or a large honeydew melon
4-5 different fruits, such as pineapple, pears, apples, grapes,
*   tangerines, lychees, strawberries, peaches and kiwi fruit*

If no canned fruit with syrup is used, dissolve the candy sugar in the water, then cool.

Slice about 2.5 cm (1 in) off the top of a melon and scoop out the flesh, discarding the seeds. Cut the flesh into small chunks. Prepare other fresh fruit, leaving it whole if small, otherwise separating into segments or cutting into small chunks.

Pour the syrup into the melon shell, then fill it up with the fruits. Cover with cling film and chill for at least 2 hours.

To serve, place the melon on top of lots of crushed ice.

Almond Float

Also known as junket, the float can be made from *agar-agar*, isinglass or gelatine. When chilled and served with a variety of fresh or canned fruit, it is a most refreshing dessert after a Chinese meal.

25 g (1 oz) agar-agar, isinglass or gelatine powder
600 ml (1 pint) water
6 tablespoons sugar
275 ml (½ pint) milk
1 teaspoon almond essence
fresh or canned mixed fruit salad with syrup (left), to serve

Dissolve the agar-agar or isinglass in about half the water in a saucepan over gentle heat; if using gelatine powder, follow the instructions on the packet. Dissolve the sugar in the remaining water in a separate saucepan. Add the milk and almond essence to the sugar mixture, then pour into a large serving bowl and mix in the agar-agar mixture. When cool, place the bowl in the refrigerator for 3-4 hours to set and chill.

To serve, cut the junket into small cubes, then pour the fruit salad and syrup over it.

Index